For Emmanuel Levinas
in homage

PHENOMENOLOGICAL EXPLANATIONS

ALPHONSO LINGIS
(Pennsylvania State University)

1986 **MARTINUS NIJHOFF PUBLISHERS**
a member of the KLUWER ACADEMIC PUBLISHERS GROUP
DORDRECHT / BOSTON / LANCASTER

Distributors

for the United States and Canada: Kluwer Academic Publishers, P.O. Box 358, Accord Station, Hingham, MA 02018-0358, USA
for the UK and Ireland: Kluwer Academic Publishers, MTP Press Limited, Falcon House, Queen Square, Lancaster LA1 1RN, UK
for all other countries: Kluwer Academic Publishers Group, Distribution Center, P.O. Box 322, 3300 AH Dordrecht, The Netherlands

Library of Congress Cataloging in Publication Data

ISBN-13: 978-90-247-3333-0 e-ISBN-13: 978-94-010-9610-2
DOI: 10.1007/978-94-010-9610-2

PHENOMENOLOGICAL EXPLANATIONS

PHAENOMENOLOGICA
COLLECTION FONDÉE PAR H.L. VAN BREDA ET PUBLIÉE SOUS LE PATRONAGE DES CENTRES D'ARCHIVES-HUSSERL

96

ALPHONSO LINGIS

PHENOMENOLOGICAL EXPLANATIONS

CONTENTS

Preface	IX
I. On Phenomenological Explanation	1
II. The Mind's Body	21
III. Being in the Interrogative Mood	41
IV. Involution in the Sensuous	59
V. The Perception of Others	73
VI. The Visible and the Vision	91
VII. Intuition of Freedom, Intuition of Law	103

PREFACE

The intentional analysis devised by phenomenology was first used to explain the meaningfulness of expressions; it aimed at exhibiting the original primary substrates that expressions refer to, and at exhibiting the subjective acts that make signs expressive. The explanation of predicative expressions was then extended to the antecedent layer of prepredicative, perceptual experiences, explaining these by locating, with peculiar kinds of immanent intuitions, the original sensile data which evidence the bodily presence of the real – and by reactivating the informing – formulating, interpreting – and the informing-forming – subjective acts that make of the sensile data, or material, perceived things.

Intentional analysis explains by decomposing the derivate references back to the original references, and by leading the mind's intentions back to the givens they refer to. Can this kind of explanation be extended? The investigations of this book have taken this question in different directions. Can phenomenological explanation be extended to exhibit not only the act-character of the mind, but its substance, its affective materiality, its locomotion, its impressed haecceity, in short, its corporeality (Chapter I)? Shall not the explanation explain that if the terra firma of being, in the maximum proximity where distance no longer introduces indeterminability, is never reached, this is not because of the defects and the finitude of our mind, but because being itself is not there as the answer, positive and affirmative – being itself is in the interrogative mood (Chapter II)? If the given being itself is in the interrogative mood, then the sensile data or material that evidence its presence are not originally "sensations" – that is, impressions, on our sensory surfaces, of sense, signs or signals of identifiable identities. How can we formulate the format of that sensuous medium, and how explain that the sensibility by which our mind is exposed to the sensuous turns into a synoptic receptivity that posits data for the formation and interpretation performed by acts of perception (Chapter III)?

Phenomenological analysis explains, secondly, by exhibiting the subjective acts that originate the giving of the data, the objectification of the objects. This transcendental direction of the analysis aims to be an eidetic science – not only to formulate the act-character of one's own mind, but that of mind in general. How is the mind of another given – in what evidences, with what acts (Chapter V)? What does it mean to intuit intuition, to see a look (Chapter VI)? An imperative weighs on the mind from the first; to explain, as to think in general, is to find oneself subject to law, or, more exactly, to the imperative for laws, the imperative for the universal and the necessary. This law, said the transcendental philosophy of Kant, is a fact. Can this fact – the first fact, for facts can be recognized as facts by a mind that thinks, that is, formulates representations of the universal and the necessary – be given in an intuition? What is the original hyle in which this fact is impressed? What is the subjective act in which, and on which, this fact is given (Chapter VII)?

CHAPTER ONE

ON PHENOMENOLOGICAL EXPLANATION

Phenomenology is to be a science of phenomena conceived to function as transcendental criticism. It is intended to elucidate the bases of scientific thought – the very fact that cognition is cognition of something given, is empirical cognition; then the nature of what is taken as given by the sciences; and the inner structure of the evidence for what is taken as given. But just exactly what is to count as phenomenological elucidation? Is it to be a simple presuppositionless, metaphysic-free intuition into the ultimate data of knowledge, achieved by a neutralizing of the theoretical sediment through which a theoretically committed mind approaches them? Or, on the contrary, is it to be a metaphysically idealist explanation of how the data of cognition originate out of transcendental constitutive consciousness, on the one hand, and out of the pretheoretical data of the *Lebenswelt*, the world of life, on the other hand? Is phenomenological elucidation intuition, or is it explanation?

1. Phenomenological Intuitionism

The great manifesto *Ideas I* declares heroically that what will be built is a philosophical discourse which from one end to the other will be grounded in immediate insight, the direct observation of what is given in evidence, and will consist nowhere of argumentation, nowhere of deduction, nowhere of induction, will not advance one sole statement that is not guaranteed by direct intuition ever available, ever repeatable.[1] Phenomenology will be resolutely anti-speculative; positivists will be criticized only for their hidden metaphysical presuppositions, for not having grounded philosophical judgments themselves in direct vision of the data.[2] It is we who are the genuine positivists, Husserl declares.[3]

To Husserl this slogan proclaims a certain conception of scientific cognition, and a certain conception of the relationship between philosophical and scientific thought. Scientific cognition alone is taken as accomplished cognition; to Husserl it is the telos of conscious life. "Scientifically judicative reason, in the manner characteristic of a highest level, presupposes all the lower levels of production effected by thinking and, when taken concretely as a theme, includes them all . . ."[4] Scientific thoughts are cognitive judgments that are grounded, whose correctness can be shown. "The scientist intends, not merely to judge, but to ground his judgments."[5] This exigency for justifications is the generating scientific intention, and builds scientific thought into rational systems. But the properly philosophical or transcendental inquiry that seeks to ground or justify the evidence for the ultimate givens of science, as well as to elucidate the nature and modalities of the evidence in which they are given, becomes a part of every science the day it carries its founding scientific intention to a grounded cognition all the way through. Philosophy is the final stage of the generating scientific will to bring cognitive thought to "radical self-understanding and fundamental self-justification; or what amounts to the same thing, to that state of being most perfectly scientific, the attainment of which is the raison d'être of philosophy . . ."[6] And if this properly philosophical task of elucidating the evidence for the primary data of science is fundamentally one, while the scientific disciplines are many, this does not mean that philosophical inquiry, although inaugurated by the exigencies of scientific reason, nonetheless acquires a certain autonomy; it rather means that when the scientific enterprise carries its exigency for rationally grounded knowledge through all the way it discovers its own fundamental unity; it means that the Renaissance founders of modern science were not wrong to believe that scientific reason was destined to build a new all-embracing *sapientia universalis*.[8]

Secondly, phenomenology is to be faithful to the fundamental commitment of positivism in that for it scientific thought means rational thought, and rational thought means not only coherent thought, thought whose assertions are grounded by rational principles – but in addition it means thought "that has the quality of insight."[9] It is the empirical thought that conceives what is given. Moments of evidence – of intuition, of simple seeing, receptivity for what is given – are the foundation for scientific thought not only in that thought begins with them and builds on them, but in that they are the authority for thought. The "principle of all principles" is that intuition is the authority for thought; that what founds, what justifies a concept is the data, which are given, and given ultimately as a matter of fact, and "simply to be accepted as they give themselves out to be, and only within the limits in which they then present themselves."[10]

Husserl's initial project was then to build a transcendental inquiry into the processes that give the ultimate data for scientific cognition which would be itself grounded in moments of intuition, and thus scientific in the positive sense of the term. He came to believe that a completely intuitionist transcendental inquiry would be possible because he believed that there are, first, moments of direct intuition into ultimate givens, out of which all knowledge arises and on which all knowledge is founded, moments of immediate contact with the "things themselves"; but that there are, secondly, also moments of direct intuition into universals, into essences; and that there are, finally, moments of direct intuition into the operations of the mind.

Phenomenology is thus established on a threefold doctrine of intuition. It begins by arguing against phenomenalism and every kind of mental immanentism that the mind is in direct, immediate contact with the things themselves; thus the doctrine of intentionality is the first foundational doctrine of phenomenology. It argues against classical empiricism that there is direct, immediate experience of idealities, essences, which is of the same nature as experience of facts, and is indeed inseparable from the experience of facts. It argues against Kantism that transcendental mental processes are not merely transcendentally deduced as the conditions for the possibility of objectivity, but can be directly intuited. For phenomenology then the transcendental mind is a living existent and particular mind, and not just the set of universal epistemological conditions presupposed by the position of objectivity.

The possibility for a phenomenology thus rests on a certain exposition of what intuition means, or, more simply, what it means that something is given, what it means to say that there are data. The phenomenological positivist thesis is not that there are three kinds of intuition; it is that there are three dimensions to every intuition – that both factuality and essentiality are given at once in an operation that makes itself visible.

The given in experience is recognized in the fact that something does not vary as the phases of mental life vary. Some term or some factor emerges that is then not a simple ingredient or correlate of a psychic state. There is something transcendent to a concrete psychic phase, something that is not extinguished when it passes, something that can recur, can make its appearance again in the next phase. *The same* something can endure. Its apparition in the antecedent moment was not necessarily but an indication, premonition, or sign of it; its reapparition in a subsequent moment not but an effect, aftereffect, or trace of its passage. It is the "thing itself"[11] immediately – that is, according to Kant's definition, intuitively – there.

But this also means that a certain ideality lies in the very givenness of everything given.[12] For being that is not exhausted in the here and now, that can be maintained the same across the shift and passage of the moment that measured its presence, that appears indefinitely reiteratable, is ideal being. The essence, which makes this recurrent form the "selfsame" thing, is also what makes it be given as the "thing itself."

Intentionality is the openness of the mind to something transcendent to it, its receptivity with regard to something given. A moment of presence passes, and the mind finds itself again before the selfsame datum: the given itself – intentionality is receptive, intuitive. But at the same time it receives the identity of what recurs the same – intentionality is an act of identification. Intuition and identification, insight into the things themselves and *Wesenschau*, essential insight, are thus, in Husserl's conception, inseparable.

And intentionality itself is a given. It identifies itself. If something can be genuinely given to a mind, if there can be a datum that is not merely a factor or an ingredient of that life, then no moment of consciousness scintillates and dies away as a singular event; each moment of presence retains or reiterates something of the moment that passes, and already anticipates something of the moment to come. The mind reiterates itself, identifies itself, recaptures itself, is given, phase by phase, to itself. That is, the intentional mind is in intuitive presence of itself.

It was then out of this three-dimensional analysis of intuition that Husserl conceived the idea of a completely intuitionist transcendental inquiry. Motivated by the intrinsically scientific exigency for grounded cognition, it would set out to make evident intuitively 1) the ultimate givens of rational cognition, 2) the ultimate principles of rational cognition, and, 3) the inner operation of the moments of evidence in which they are given.

But immediate insight, intuitive clarity, is not forthwith achieved. For if all scientific cognition indeed presupposes data taken as given, still scientific thought consists in the theoretical elaboration and interpretation of those data, and in the theoretically determined data there are interpretative, theoretical presuppositions involved – idealizing, universalizing presuppositions. In addition the metaphysical presupposition of the antecedent reality of the natural world is inevitably involved in all positive judicative thought, since to know data means to take data to be systematically connected (given within a world), and to be there, to be existent, and only thus given for cognition. An inquiry into the givenness of a world, a mode of givenness antecedent to all thought, will be required. The world functions as the horizon in which all given data are intuited; the position of every given involves a suppostion of a world in which data figure. In order that the mode of givenness of the world be itself scrutinized, it is necessary that its ever-concomitant supposition be neutralized. And this turns out to be a very difficult operation. The world is always inevitably operative as the continual abiding field in which something can be maintained the same across the passage of time or across a succession of thought operations; it is always inevitably operative during every rational or insightful thought. How then is it to cease to be operative, in order to be given? How is the mode of givenness of a world to be intuitively elucidated?

Thus the intuitionist enterprise, which at first sight seems like simplicity itself, encounters the difficulties of desedimenting the theoretical interpretative elaborations from the primary data of rational thought, and the difficulty of neutralizing the supposition of a real world ever already operative as soon as something is taken as given. A battery of techniques and stratagems, and criteria, will have to be elaborated, and the moment of the expected intuitive elucidation deferred.

2. Phenomenological Explanation

But these difficulties which obstruct the intuitionist procedure already delineate a second, and quite different, meaning of phenomenological elucidation, according to which what is properly phenomenological has the form of a return to the original, to the origin – to the original insights into the world behind the theoretical elaborations, to the original worldstructure given before the data are given. Here is what we can identify as the Humean inspiration of phenomenology: that in the world of thought it is the original that is clear, and the way to elucidate is to return to the origin. If by thought-procedure we mean either analysis, that is, breakdown of the complex into its constituent parts; or we mean comprehension, that is, scrutiny of the properties of the complex as such, its internal order and organization; or else we mean explanation, that is, seeing something in the light of its origin, seeing what caused it, what produced it, seeing from what principles or from what cause it originates – then this second line of phenomenological investigation is explanatory.

However, this return to the origin, to the original, shall have two different meanings in phenomenology.

a. Return to the Subjective Origin

On the one hand, elucidation of the foundations of science by way of a return to the origin of constituted thought means a scrutiny of the inner life of the cognitive subjectivity. Husserl derives from Bolzano the decisive character of the distinction between the judging *act* and the *judgment* itself, and, in general, between the performance of consciousness, the moment of evidence, on the one hand, and the object of consciousness, the object given in that moment of evidence, on the other hand. This distinction is a distinction between the origin and the constituted; Husserl says that phenomenology is built on that distinction. A judgment is not a living mental operation; it is a sort of ideal object that can be maintained the same before a mind that deals with it in a succession of different operations, and at different times. But to radically understand a judgment is to understand the scope of the judging intentionality that was its constitutive, productive origin.

When we examine Husserl's most fully elaborated samples of what he takes to be phenomenological elucidation of the foundations of science, they turn out most often to be explanations of this kind, explanations of bodies of constituted thought in terms of their origin in the subjective life, elucidations of judgments and bodies of judgments in terms of the judging intentionality that was their constitutive, productive origin. Thus when Husserl sets out to argue that the total formal science, the *mathesis universalis*, has two sides: a formal apophantics, on the one hand, that is, a formal theory of the pure forms of cognition – of judgments, arguments, and theories – and, on the other hand, a formal mathematics, which is a formal theory of the forms of any object of cognition whatever, of formal multiplicities and of the forms of operations performable on pure object-forms and multiplicity-forms – he sets out to show that this distinction between a formal apophantics and a formal mathematics reflects the two intentions involved in scientific cognitive life.[13]

In its primary phase cognitive thought posits or determines objects of thought, that is, takes them to be such and such. But that first means: takes them *to be* such and such, takes them to be, posits them as existing. This is thought governed by the theoretical interest: it is the will to know what is. There can be a purely formal science of the forms of the objects of thought and of the forms of the relationships between them; that science is formal mathematics. Mathematical thought, then, does not originate as a simple construction of deductive systems with emptied signs; it arises as an elaboration of a purely formal science of the pure forms of any object whatever, any object thought may posit as existing: it is formal ontology, formal science of the forms of existence.[14] But now in a second phase, the critical phase, thought suspends its original position of existence, and treats it now as a *supposition* of existence.[15] Critical thought is that moment of hesitation, of scrupule, that always accompanies truly scientific thinking. It is thought governed by an interest for verification. It attends to just what it was that was supposed in order to see if what was originally supposed can be verified. The critical reflex in scientific thought produces attention to supposition as such; the formal science of the forms of supposition – formal apophantics – corresponds then to the cognitive intention governed by the interest in verification.[16]

When Husserl sets out to argue that the complete formal apophantics will be an edifice of three separate disciplines: a pure morphology of judgment-forms, a formal theory of the forms of argument, and a formal theory of the forms of theories – and, then, that the formal theory of the forms of argument and the formal theory of the forms of theories have two parallel elaborations: as a coherence or consequence logic, and as a truth-logic, he will justify this articulation of formal science likewise by an elucidation of the phases of cognitive thought. The justification will consist in showing how, in cognitive life, there arise different intentions: the intention to form and maintain a judgment, the intention to maintain a sequence of judgments such that it does not cancel itself out as it proceeds, and the intention to form a body of judgment-sequences about a body of thematic objects.[17]

The *Formal and Transcendental Logic* is elaborated to show thus that to understand what logic is it is not enough to know to operate logic, but it is also not enough just to see, to intuit, what the logical entities are; it is necessary to see how logical formations originate in the cognitive life, out of the very performance of a thought that means to determine a world scientifically. The next book Husserl will work on on logic, *Experience and Judgment*, will be subtitled

"Research for a Genealogy of Logic."

This is transcendental criticism very much in the spirit of Kantism, with two key differences: on the one hand Husserl does not simply deduce the subjective operations involved from an examination of their objective results, that is, from an examination of the forms of objectivity; he claims to elucidate the subjective operations of cognition by direct insight. His method is to "reactivate" the fundamental, founding subjective operations, and study their nature during the course of an intuitive attention to them at work.

And as a result (this is the second difference) Husserl believes that a procedure of this kind, returning to the moments of the subjective life in which objects were given and took form, reactivating those founding moments, may yield new light on the fundamental data. This kind of transcendental critique would be able to purify and stabilize shifting intentions in the moments of evidence that gave the objects of the fundamental concepts of science. For example, this method alone will be able to show how formal mathematical thought arises and what is its meaning, will be able to show the origin of the truth-axioms of logical theory.

Husserl believes that this kind of transcendental critique will be able to make positive contributions within the body of science itself. For him Kant's philosophy does not build into scientific thought; it consists in taking the universe of science as given, taking the universe of objectivity as already constituted by the universal laws of objective thought, and then saying that the universal laws that form objectivity are in fact subjective forms, or, more exactly, formative operations of transcendental subjectivity. Subjectivity is specified, in Kantism, simply as the set of universal a priori formative operations which impose on the representation of the objective universe the universal forms it has. One can then address to such an explanation the criticism Hume addressed to all explanations that explain the origin of this world by appealing to God's creative activity; if you do not see God directly, all you can do is set up God as a cause who can account for the world because he precontains in himself pre-eminently all those perfections, but just those perfections, which we find in this world. Such an explanation consists in doubling up the world with an alleged cause who is just the mirror image of the world on the plane of the inobservable.[18] In the same way it is hard to see what we have really gained by explaining, as Kantism does, that the objective representation of the universe has its origin in subjectivity if subjectivity is not directly intuited, but rather its a priori forms read off from the constituted structure of the objective world, deduced out of the characteristics of objectivity. Then the very same universal forms are the universal laws of objectivity as well as the a priori forms of subjectivity; the objective universe is doubled up with a subjectivity in its image and likeness, which is allegedly its origin, that is, its existence before its existence.

Transcendental criticism for Husserl too is a procedure taking already constituted scientific formations, and tracing them back to the moments of subjectivity in which they were constituted. But for him the transcendental grounding does not start by taking the sciences as they are given, and end by leaving the sciences illuminated from beneath, or rather reflected in the mirror of subjectivity, but intact. On the contrary the transcendental procedure as Husserl conceives it is a veritably constructive scientific movement; it begins by taking the bodies of science as they are constituted by purely objective thought, but in reactivating the inaugural moments of evidence that originally give the data of those sciences the transcendental elucidation can purify and reform those evidences, and institute these purified objects as norms and standards, purge the latent ambivalence of fundamental terms, and thus send back into the body of science itself a line of reform. "Everywhere we observe," he complains, "the repeatedly cited error of accepting the sciences as something that already exists – as though inquiry into foundations signified only an ex post facto clarification, or, at most, an improvement that would not essentially alter these sciences themselves. The truth is that sciences that have paradoxes, that operate with fundamental concepts not produced by the work of originary clarification and criticism, are not sciences at all, but, with all their ingenious performances, mere theoretical techniques."[19] The return to the origin in subjectivity is to be a genuinely "creative" return. What is to be created is the autojustification which transforms theoretical techniques into genuine understanding and self-understanding – what is created is the authentically scientific dignity of thought.

To return to the origin of science, of thought products, in subjectivity is to go back to the moments of evidence that give the inaugural objects of rational thought. But to retrieve and reactivate these founding operations of subjectivity is not to awaken intuitions immediately; a methodology will be required, because, Husserl says, the subjective moments that give objects, that objectify, operate anonymously or "unconsciously."[20] While it is effectively at work the subjective operation hides itself with what it makes evident; the operation is hidden by the object it makes visible. The exhibited, the intuited, hides the exhibiting. Thus this time the intuition obstructs the explanation; what is given in intuition hides its origin.

b. Genetic Analysis of Meaning

There is a second meaning to phenomenological elucidation taken as return to the origin – what Husserl calls "genetic analysis of meaning." It belongs to the last elaboration of his work.

Meaning turns out to be a crossroads of references. If something has meaning, it refers on ahead to some object, state of objects, or nexus of relationships. For the meaning to be clear is here for it to lead one's attention to those signified terms; it is the epiphany of the things themselves that produces the light that clarifies the meaning.[21] To clarify meaning is to produce the corresponding intuition into the things meant. Or, in Husserl's terminology, it is to fulfill the empty intentions of meaning. Phenomenological elucidation in its first sense, as intuition, is clarification conceived in these terms.

But in addition constituted meaning also "points back," back to the productive constitutive subjectivity that gives it. For if it is true that we could proceed like Kant, starting by taking the thought products, the scientific judgments and theories, as given, as before us, and deduce the productive acts of subjectivity that gave them, that implies that somehow on the thought products themselves there is an indication, a trace, that points back to the moment of consciousness that brought them forth. If it is true that we could proceed as Husserl does, starting with the thought products, judgments and theories as evident, and reactivate just those types of conscious acts that gave them originally, then somehow on the thought products themselves there is an indication, a pointing back, a retroreference to their origin in subjectivity. All we have are the sedimented thought-products of Euclid; but they themselves will show us how to rekindle, in our own minds, the very living thought performances that once moved in the mind of Euclid.[22]

There is yet another dimension of retroreference involved in constituted meanings: that whereby it points back to other meanings that preceded it, with which it was elaborated or on which it was founded. Thus "the red" points back to the original predicate "red" which was nominalized to produce the thematic substrate "the red." "The similarity" points back to the original relation "similar" which was nominalized to produce it. Universal judgments point back to the singular judgments out of which they were produced by syntactical transformation. Syntactically compounded judgments point back to syntactically uncompounded, primitive judgments. Judgments that modalize existence point back to categorical judgments that originally posit existence. Judgments that refer to objects in their absence point back to judgments that determine objects in their presence; that is, to judicative acts within which the data themselves were given, experiential judgments. In them the observation – that is, the very vision, the perception – of what is given is conceived, is first determined for thought.

By this kind of analysis Husserl holds that it is possible to trace all judgments within the body of a science, syntactical transformation by syntactical transformation, back to the primitive judgments, the experiential judgments, that posit individual objects, that determine the given objects of which this science is a discourse. This kind of analysis exhibits science as a body of statements that form a true hierarchy, founded on one another, such that the foundational judgments are judgments about individuals of the world first given. These will be shown to be given in prepredicative experiences within the horizon of the antecedently given world – the world antecedent to all thought: what Husserl names, in his last period, the *Lebenswelt*, the world of life.

This is reduction to the original in a new sense; Husserl names it "genetic analysis of meaning." "Judgments, as the finished products of a 'constitution' or 'genesis,' can and must be asked about this genesis. The essential peculiarity of such products is precisely that they are senses that bear within them, as a sense-implicate of their genesis, a sort of historicalness; that in them, level by level, sense points back to original sense . . . and therefore each sense-formation can be asked about its *essentially necessary sense-history*."[23]

Phenomenology now speaks of an "origin" and "genesis" of meanings; idealities bear within themselves "a sort of historicalness." How can meaning, which is meaning by being selfsame, ideally identical, transtemporal, have also an "essentially necessary sense-history"? Is this not historicism, taking the deathless ideas to have been born, and thus divesting them, by birthright, of their claim to validity and normativity? It would seem that now to understand a meaning is no longer to produce an intuition that brings what was meant into immediate presence; it is rather to retrace an evolution of references as such.

3. Explanatory Intuition and Intuitive Explanation

Are these two directions of phenomenological elucidation complementary – or incompossible? On the one hand, rational thought is thought grounded by insight; fulfilled cognition can only mean intuition, and phenomenology is to be entirely intuitive from one end to the other. Phenomenology's principle of all principles is that intuition alone is genuine and founded cognition. And Husserl's primary terminology for the phases of cognitive life is contrived to reflect this conviction: there is "empty" intentionality and there is "fulfilled" intentionality – filled with the very light of the things themselves, immediately present, given, evident. Fulfilled cognition is the telos of intentionality: intentionality is the very essence of the mind; the mind then is teleologically destined for the immediate presence of the extramental. To understand is to see – not a conceptual entity, a mental representation, but the intended things themselves; to understand a concept, a theory, a science, is to achieve intuition of the things themselves designated by that concept, meant by that theory, by that science. And to understand understanding is to see the operations of understanding at work. Husserl sets out to do Kant one better: to make sure that intuition and understanding do not for a moment separate, even in the discussion about intuition and about understanding.

But on the other hand, to understand is to explain, to trace back the given to its origin – to its origin in subjectivity, and to its origin in a prior given antecedent to cognition and on which it is founded. To understand a judgment is not just to see the things themselves it determines to be there; it is also to see that judgment as originating in subjectivity, in a judging, and, on the other hand, it is to see that that judgment originated in another judgment, an experiential judgment, and finally in a prepredicative moment of experience. Phenomenological analysis is here a recovery of the hidden, of the concealed. The origin always turns out to be hidden. Phenomenological analysis returns from the given, from what is exhibited in a moment of evidence, to a scrutiny of the operation of the exhibiting, which, Husserl says, operates "anonymously," hidden by the very given it exhibits. And, secondly, the genetically original determinations of thought are hidden, hidden by thoughts that are founded on them. The structure of the accomplished body of thought in a science hides the primitive experiental judgments on which that thought was founded, hides the moments of prepredicative experience that originally gave the objects of that science out of the *Lebenswelt*, the world of life. There is a growing obscurity in the ever more consistently and completely evident elaborations of scientific explanation. To the point that practicing mathematicians in the twentieth century could be no longer able to say what the originally given mathematical entities are, or in what experiences they were given.

Husserl declares on the one hand that elucidation is clarification, is exposure to the light, the primordial light, that of being itself, the clarity of the things themselves. But on the other hand he says that it is an uncovering of what is hidden by those luminous givens; it is an effort to expose the hidden and anonymous operations of primary consciousness, and it is an effort to expose and bring to light the original data given in the primary experiences of the world and now hidden by the very thoughts built on them.

It is the plenary fullness of the things themselves, which fulfill intuition, that hides their origins. It is the light itself that hides – the primary light, that of presence itself. The light illuminates, makes being phosphorescent, but also hides its own source, dazzles.

There is then in the practice of the phenomenological kind of elucidation an internal discordance. We are not surprised that those who have tried to think what Husserl thought have so often come to the conviction that his idea of the mind, and consequently his idea of elucidation, are metastable amalgams, which come apart in the exercise. Are there not two phenomenologies, or two intentions in phenomenology: a descriptive or explicative method, intuitive, metaphysically neutral, proceeding after the phenomenological epochè, which method is destined to reveal the given itself – and an explanatory method, metaphysically idealist, endeavoring to account for scientific truth in terms of experience of the world, and endeavoring to account for the world in terms of consciousness? But for Husserl to do phenomenology is to know in practice how it is that when you elucidate you intuit and you explain, that your intuition is your explanation and your explanation is your intuition. Because the meaning of something is that crossroads of references – references ahead, to the given, references back to subjectivity, retroreferences to an origin of meaning in a world antecedent to all thought – then to see what is meant is indeed to see these very references and retroreferences. If one can return to the origin it is because the way is marked out and still visible on what is now present; it is because, like a fossil, everything brought into presence still bears with itself the traces and smell of its origins. To see it is then to see where it came from. To return to its origin is to go back to see the origin. Thus to see what is there is to reconstitute the genealogy of the present; to see the present is to see the traces of a history.

4. Mind as Intuition and as Constitution

If phenomenological elucidation proceeds by reactivating moments of evidence – and especially the founding moments of evidence that institute rational thought – the inner discordance we find in this elucidation and this uncovering we find in the moment of evidence itself. Husserl describes the moment of evidence both in terms of intuition, immediate insight, pure givenness of the object itself – and also in terms of origination, constitution of the object. To understand what Husserl means by mind is to think these two terms as one – to think that intuition is production and that production is intuition.

In declaring that intentionality is the essence of consciousness, Husserl meant to say that the mind is essentially intuitive; that intuition of the given is "primal consciousness," "the universal preeminent form of consciousness ... to which the whole life of consciousness is teleologically destined."[24] Intuition is the moment of evidence taken as a simple giving of the object itself, or better, it is the pure givenness of the object, the epiphany of the object as it itself is.

But, on the other hand, the event of evidence is also described as an act, a performance, or an operation. The giving of the object is called its constitution. Husserl explains that constitution is not creation, but it is "in all seriousness" a production.[25] It is a formative activity, or a praxis. But, he says, *"this manner of givenness – givenness as coming out of a productive activity* – is nothing other than *the sort of 'perception' proper to given data."*[26] In the event of evidence, being is founded, instituted, produced. This compound of concepts requires us to refuse the Aristotelian and Kantian identification of receptivity with passivity; here receptivity is activity, intuition is institution. By its own activity the mind is afflicted with something alien, something given.

The model of this conception of mind is to be found in Husserl's analysis of cognition as enacted in judication. To know is to enact relationship with an object. Husserl rejects every idea that cognition begins by enacting a relationship with something other than the object itself – with a sign of the object, or an effect of the object in the mind. Attention to the mental conception of an object is a secondary development, that arises out of a primary attention to the object itself. The primary thought makes contact with something given, and posits it as existing, and determines it as existing thus and so. It is the critical scruple, the moment of skeptical hesitation, that suspends the primary position of existence and treats the objects originally posited as suppositions, as mental conceptions of objects. The critical moment is the cause of that mental diplopia that doubles up the objects with mental representations of objects. But a judgment taken as a subjective supposition presupposes the original contact with the judged object or state of affairs.

The moment of contact with something given must have occurred at the start. But this simplest form of cognition is already an activity, an articulation. A determinate object is given in predication whereby something is taken to be there, posited, maintained present, and then specified in some fashion. And in being posited as existing in one moment but then maintained, posited as existing in another moment, in another judicative moment, existing the same, an object emerges in its existent objectivity. This is what makes the *object itself* – something determinate, something abiding and identifiable – be given to a mind. Cognition begins not as a creation of an object, but as a making contact with an object, a positing of something as existing, as there. But predication takes a content *as existing*. Thus a predication is an intuition, and intuition is a predicative performance. Judicative cognition is the primitive form of cognition, and it is analyzed as a formative activity, which determines something taken to be there. In this formative activity what comes to pass is that contact has been made immediately with the object itself. Intuition, that is, the immediate presence of the given to a mind, is enacted in a predicative operation.

In Husserl's program for the genetic analysis of meanings the decisive role of this analysis becomes clear to us. Husserl believes that all thoughts, all judgments, can be reduced to ultimate predicative judgments that determine individual objects of the world. Thus if all scientific thought thinks what is given, it is in predication that something is given to a mind. All cognitive thought-products will have to be elucidated by being traced back to reality-giving perceptual predications.

In Husserl's phenomenology the intuition, the vision, that preceded predication was already predication *avant la lettre*. The primitive judgments of a science are experiental judgments. He writes "experience itself functions in and not beside the original judgments."[27] But this also means that phenomenology will seek in prepredicative experience an origin of the very forms of predication. "This ... is the place systematically, *starting from judgment, to discover* that certainty and modalities of certainty, suppositive intention and fulfillment, identical existent and identical sense, evident having of something itself, trueness of being (being 'actual') and truth as correctness of sense – that *none of these is a peculiarity exclusively within the predicative sphere, that, on the contrary, they all belong already to the intentionality of experience.*"[28]

With this affirmation Husserl initiates an interpretation of perception according to the model of judgment. Perception will be seen as an act in which contact is made with an individual object, and in which that object is determinate somehow, receiving some quasi-predicative determination out of the act of turning to it and making contact with it. Object-constitution originally means perception as an act of predication. Perception is an act that maintains something the same across the various moments of sensual experience. Thus to perception the object itself is given, the selfsame object. And perception involves the taking of what one sees as existing; seeing is believing. This taking something to be existent is a kind of assertion; it has its syntax. For perception does not open upon a medly of sensations, but upon forms, configurations, groups, patterns. The perceptual activity too then determines objects according to different typical syntactical forms, just as judicative thought does. The perceptual field is already syntactically structured, already punctuated, already phrased by the activity that originally gives it, intuits it.

Once we have seen this, we can raise questions about this pre-predicative perception, this perception Husserl takes to be already working predicatively. Is perception an ascription of predicates, an interpretation of sensa taken as data? Is it a function by which the mind informs itself? Is it not also a function that informs, that shapes, a materiality? Does the mind not have to be a substance that moves, and feels itself moving, in order to index successive sensuous patterns as perspectival aspects of abidingly identifiable things? And is taking something as existing really a predicative operation – is it not first a shaping of the sensile material in one's own sensibility into patterns? Do we not have to reopen the inspection of the mind's act, when it constitutes something as intuited? How far can we go by way of achieving intuitive insight not only into the act, but into the reality of the mind?

Notes

1. Edmund Husserl, *Ideas Pertaining to a Pure Phenomenology and to a Phenomenological Philosophy*, First Book, trans. F. Kersten (The Hague: Martinus Nijhoff, 1982), pp. 167–70.
2. Ibid., pp. 37–39.
3. Ibid., p. 39.
4. Edmund Husserl, *Formal and Transcendental Logic*, trans. Dorion Cairns (The Hague: Martinus Nijhoff, 1969), p. 28.
5. Ibid.
6. Ibid., p. 153.
7. Ibid., p. 4.
8. Ibid.
9. Ibid., p. 18.
10. *Ideas* I, p. 44.
11. *Formal and Transcendental Logic*, pp. 156–62.
12. Ibid., pp. 163–64.
13. Ibid., pp. 120–26.
14. Ibid., pp. 72–89.
15. Ibid., pp. 122–24.
16. Ibid., p. 126.
17. Ibid., pp. 179–81.
18. David Hume, *An Inquiry Concerning Human Understanding* (New York: Liberal Arts Press, 1955), pp. 145–49.
19. *Formal and Transcendental Logic*, p. 34.
20. Ibid., p. 34.
21. *Ideas* I, pp. 153–55.
22. Edmund Husserl, *The Crisis of European Sciences and Transcendental Phenomenology*, trans. David Carr (Evanston: Northwestern University Press, 1970), pp. 353–78.
23. *Formal and Transcendental Logic*, p. 208.
24. *Ideas* I, p. 36.
25. *Formal and Transcendental Logic*, p. 167.
26. Ibid., p. 168.
27. Ibid., p. 209.
28. Ibid., pp. 209–10.

CHAPTER TWO

THE MIND'S BODY

> The soul's reality is based upon corporeal matter, not the latter upon the soul.
>
> *Ideen* III

By absolute consciousness Husserl did not mean to designate simply an epistemological function; absolute consciousness is a region of reality, albeit the proto-region, an ontic term, an existent, individualizing itself in its internal temporality as a singular ego. In addition it inheres in a body.[1] Psychism is apperceived in the heart of nature. Conversely corporeity is apperceived within intentionality itself.

1. Consciousness Naturalized in a Body

Bodies are discovered in the course of our survey of transcendent nature. They occupy sites in nature's space and time – the time which is physically measured.[2] They are empirical unities of nature, given primordially in sensory perspectives, and elaborated in the empirical-objective investigation pursued in the natural sciences. These things (*Körper*) are animated by the reification or naturalization of consciousness. (Husserl does not first seek the operation of consciousness in bodies by seeking to unravel the experience I have of my own consciousness at work in my own body – the *corps propre* of Sartre and Merleau-Ponty.)[3]

The fully transcendent, empirical naturalness of bodies makes them able to function as supports for an emergence of psychism in nature. Bodies appear perspectively as "sensible schemata" connected circumstantially-causally to concomitantly varying natural things of their environments, and eventually to the whole of nature. During these sensible apparations and systematically connected to them, there is apperceived the non-perspectival stream of psychic states open to empirical observation with the methods of psychology. Husserl admits two sorts of connections between corporeal states and these psychic properties: psychic properties such as sensations, affects, impulses can be functionally linked to corporeal states as to their conditions, or corporeal movements may be functionally linked to psychic sequences as their expressions.[4] The psychic "properties" – functions, aptitudes, character traits, dispositions – inhere in an ego-substrate which, if not given perspectively,[5] is nonetheless manifested progressively in the course of apparition of psychic properties[6] as a unity which is not that of a sensible schema but of a stream – a temporal rather than a spatial Gestalt. The psyche is a real (realized) ego-subject, a self-identical empirical unity manifested in individual real properties, "interwoven" (*verflochten*) with nature in that the course of psychic properties is systematically linked to bodily "circumstances" (*Umstände*) by a "functionality regulated by laws."

Thus natural, objectal corporeity, by a sort of overdetermination of properties, supports upon itself a certain manifestation – an appresentation – of psychism in the sphere of transcendence. But the psychism "interwoven" with bodies, "functionally linked" to bodily circumstances, is not presented simply to the perceptual intention that primally opens upon, gives, nature. The movement transgressing bodily appearances toward their "appresented" psychic properties requires, in addition, the lateral operation of empathy (*Einfühlung*).[7] The intentionality that discerns, apperceives, consciousness in nature interwoven with bodies does so on the basis of the resemblance of those bodies with the body with which it is itself interwoven. There was first an intimate experience of a union of the corporeal with the intentional within, which was then, across the phenomenon of spontaneous corporeal association (*Paarung*) transferred (*überträgt sich*) to all analogous bodies in nature.

The animation of bodies in nature, observed in natural perception, thus answers to a corporeity of consciousness, to be discovered within by transcendental reflection. No doubt it sounds strange to speak of an incarnation of consciousness in this philosophy, whose unremitting intention is to free the theory of knowledge from every kind of naturalism by regressing to the sphere of pure or absolute consciousness, where the essence of mentality is intentionality, and where intentionality is not any kind of movement of or from one real being to another (for example, from the subject to the object), but is the purely ideal "movement" ascribing flux to identity, givenness to ideality – movement from the sensible to the intelligible. Yet corporeity appears impossible to conjure, and reappears, in a totally denaturalized and deobjectified incidence, after all the reductions, within the absolute sphere itself, as the incarnation of absolute consciousness. It is this "absolute" corporeity that seems to us the most extraordinary of Husserl's findings regarding the role of the body. For a philosophy of incarnate consciousness is not genuinely formulated by asserting that consciousness moves a body (living and operating on the outside, in the spectacle of nature), or that a body is the vehicle of consciousness, but by showing, or discovering, by reflexive examination of reduced consciousness, how corporeity is implicated in the internal structure of consciousness.

What then is the intimate experience of corporeity that consciousness knows within itself?

2. The Emergence of Corporeity in the Sphere of Absolute Consciousness

In three ways Husserl comes upon a certain corporeity – nowise objectified, nowise naturalized, nowise transcendent – implicated within the absolute sphere itself, implicated in the very operation of intentional constitution.

1. A certain corporeity of the subject is discovered in the object-structure of objects – not as component or ingredient of objects, but as a factor of the objectivity-structure *with which* or according to which consciousness constitutes objects. Husserl uncovers such

acorporeity of the subject in that a) the things are relative to a body in the polarity of their orientation, and also in that b) "real" and "unreal" properties of things are relative to a set of normal or abnormal "states" of the subject which are an inevitable part of the total context of "circumstances" within which sensorial appearances vary and things take form as invariants.

a) The object-unity of things is intended across the series of perspectival sensuous apparitions. A disparate succession of apparitions can motivate and legitimize their coalescence into an object-unity because the intrinsic structure and grain of each is compatible with and conforms with that of the others. But in addition disparate sensible apparitions caught across different moments of time can be apparitions of different sides of one and the same thing because each is an apparition of that thing from a different point of view. Each has an *index of orientation.* Each aspect refers to other aspects by referring to a center of orientation that refers to a system of other centers of orientation within which this center has identity. Thus the constitution of objects requires a subject's intentionality that is situated somewhere – within the very space it constitutes. And the ascription of a multiplicity of sensible apparitions oriented differently to one object-identity requires that the situatedness of intentionality be variable.[8]

This situatedness and free mobility of consciousness is felt within consciousness itself in the form of kinesthetic sensations. Husserl does not treat kinesthetic sensations as discrete representations or motor images of body movements recorded or reflected in the immobility of subjectivity. The field of kinesthetic sensations is part of the total system of moving "circumstances" in the midst of which poles of object-identity take form; they supply the orientation-index which motivates the coalescence of a series of sensible appearances into one object.[9] Thus they function not as representations of objects (such as one's own body-object), but as motivational factors for the objectification of (transcendent) objects. Kinesthetic sensations make felt, within the sphere of consciousness, the relativity of each perceptual profile to a certain orientation. They reveal that the intentionality that means or intends an object is also a movement of orientation with regard to that object.

If I move my eyes, my hand, my stance, I acquire other views of the things: each profile is oriented in a context of possible movements and possible positions. The awareness of this motivational structure is not the performance of a reasoning; it is the kinesthetic awareness of a free variability of orientation, the free mobility of the subject, motivating the coalescence of a series of views into one object.[10] The "if ... then ..." significance of kinestheses is how they are kinesthetic and not representational.[11] But by already meaning "if ... then ...," they dispense with the necessity of explicit reasoning. Indeed such reasoning would be possible only if the appearances one reasons about (reasoning that these compatible appearances are appearances of one, and not several, chairs) are already kinesthetically given as oriented with respect to one's own position.

Thus the crystallization of object-units out of a dispersion of differently oriented sensorial apparitions cannot fail to reveal a kinesthetic field, functioning in the constitution of every object. The field of kinesthetic sensations is not a representation, within the subject, of a materiality; it is disclosure of the materiality of subjectivity. It reveals subjectivity itself as oriented, already turning in the very space it will constitute by constituting objects.[12]

b) The corporeity of the subject is also revealed in the difference between the constitution of real objects, objects really perceived, and simulacra or phantasms. For this difference involves a difference between normal and anomalous "states" of the perceiver.

The invariant structure of a sensible thing is discerned in the course of sensorial apparitions varying in function of the context of "circumstances" (*Umstände*). The color-tone of appearances varies with the ambient light, the sharpness of contour with the direction of the light, the resonance with the relative silence of the field. But certain variations cannot be ascribed to circumstances given in the phenomenal field, and thus, not integrated into the field of determinable phenomenal links, do not acquire solid reality, remain phantasmal.[13] When they are affected, compensated for or eliminated, by changes of position or attitude, they are rejected from the system of sensorial properties of a thing and ascribed to the material state of the subject. "With each flutter of my eyelashes a curtain lowers and rises, though I do not think for an instant of imputing this eclipse to the things themselves; with each movement of my eyes that sweep the space before me the things suffer a brief torsion, which I also ascribe to myself; and when I walk in the street with eyes fixed on the horizon of the houses, the whole of the setting near at hand quivers with each footfall on the asphalt, then settles down in its place."[14] The underbrush of sensorial phantasms are denounced as such by the "true" apparition of the things, and disclose the set of subjective adjustments that will conjure them from the world. These adjustments are not adjustments of a hypothetic *Sinngebung* being repudiated by the non-compatibility of a series of sensible appearances; they are rather material adjustments, adjustments of position, stance, or state. In these adjustments, and in the necessity for them, there arises the evidence of a state of normal corporeity of the subjectivity ("psychophysical conditionality"),[15] which is subject to anomalous states.

Thus the possibility of intending objects across the flux of sensorial apparitions involves corporeity in the guise of a "position" and "state" of the subject. Consciousness is localized in this position and in this "state." The localization of consciousness, implicated by the panorama of the things, is revealed within by the states Husserl names *Empfindnisse*.[16] *Empfindnisse* are states of contact – touch, pressure, heat, cold – and of "being moved" in both the kinesthetic and the affective sense – states of tension and relaxation, pleasure, pain, agreeableness, etc. They are states in which the distinction between subjective act and aimed-at object, between the feeling "act" and the felt "content," is not discernible; in them an ambivalent sensoriality reflects both the sensible qualities that announce the presence of a transcendent thing and the sensitivity of the perceiver localized in an "extensivity." *Empfindnisse* "spread out" from within in an extensivity (*Ausbreitung*) of sensorial content which contrasts with the extension (*Ausdehnung*) of the transcendent objects intended across them.[17] They reveal consciousness in a voluminousness, in hands that feel the heat, feet that feel the cold, fingers that feel the relief and grain of things;[18] they reveal consciousness as a sensitivity that inhabits organs that move.

This first analysis of the meaning of corporeity in consciousness has been exterior and retrogressive; it proceeds by surveying the field of objectivity in which objects take form, and in discovering a subject-corporeality as part of the "circumstances" which form the context of every object. Corporeity here means that every consciousness of a space of objects has itself a position within that space, and every consciousness of real things and of phantasms has a normal, and an anomalous, "state." Attention to the ambivalent *Empfindnisse* reveals an internal experience of the consciousness localized in that position and state.

2. If we turn now to the Husserl explanation of intentionality we shall discover an incidence of corporeity revealed through direct reflection on the *essence* of consciousness.

Object are the telos of consciousness; they are attained in intuition, wherein their "carnal" (*leibhaft*) presence is immediately *given*. But for them to be given is not for objects to be received into some receptacle; consciousness orients itself toward objects, and is synthetically receptive of them, inasmuch as it posits or presumes (*meinen*) the ideal identities regulating the differentiation of their sensorial aspects. The *givenness* of the object is in the ideal identity that is maintained and affirmed across the flux of conscious attitudes and states in its regard.

But objects are (perhaps always[19]) intended across the materiality of hyletic data. Hyletic data are "sensations." They are intra-psychic; they belong to the sphere of reduced consciousness, and can be discerned by a kind of reflection.[20]

Husserl has not, with his concept of intentionality, forged a new and unitary concept of the essence of mind; in it he has conjoined a hylomorphic conception of the mind – undermined – with a hermeneutic conception of the mind – undermined. Despite Gurwitsch and Sartre, intentionality does not obviate all postulation of sensations; sensations are implicated in both conceptions that the concept of intentionality conjoins in its original fashion. On the one hand, the "sensations," the hyletic data, are mental "material"; they are to intentionality as matter is to form, and intentionality constitutes objects by "animating" (*beseelen, durchgeistigen*) this matter. Intentionality is the formative animation of psychic matter. And yet the patterns of hyletic matter (they do form "patterns"[21]) animated by the intentional operation of the mind, forming "representatives" of things in the mind, in no way form "mental representations" of things; it is not these patterns that the mind knows, consciousness is not consciousness *of* these hyletic patterns. The objects of consciousness are not representations formed, shaped, out of this matter. Here is the fundamental difference between the phenomenological and the empiricist conceptions of sensations.

On the other hand, Husserl uses a hermeneutic schema of the mind – undermined. He says that intentionality is an "interpretation" (*Deutung*) of sensations in the mind, "taking them to mean" the presence of transcendent objects. The "movement" of intentionality which goes forth unto the things themselves is the purely ideal movement of interpretation of intrapsychic data. It is the purely ideal movement which presumes or posits (*meinen*) poles of ideal identity across the streams of sense data, taking the sensorial as adumbrations of something intelligible. Yet this "interpretation" is peculiar in that the data "interpreted" are not first given in themselves. It is because they are not themselves given that hyletic data can be "taken as" the *immediate* evidence of the presence of transcendent objects. (This is what keeps the phenomenological explanation from being an intellectualist conception of perception.)

The hyletic materiality is required both by the Husserlian conception of things and by the Husserlian conception of consciousness. In casting these *Abschattungen*, these shadows, on the substance of the mind, things announce their carnal (*leibhaft*) presence – as "bodies" present to some-body. And the nature of their identity – presumed, meant, but presumed on the basis of data – requires the duality of a transcendent ideality and an intra-psychic impact.

While both the hylomorphic and the hermeneutic conceptions of the mind are maintained, conjoined, and undermined in Husserl's conception of the operation of intentionality, neither can be conceived without the intervention of sensations, hyletic matter. The Husserlian intentionality animates/interprets a mental materiality without making of it any kind of tableau; materiality affects, encumbers the Husserlian consciousness and makes of it not just an epistemological function, but life, *Erlebnis*, experience lived through. The hyletic substance is the *corps de l'esprit* (Valéry), a corporeity *of* intentionality.

3. Starting with the object-body perceived in the sphere of transcendence, moving to the corporeity that appears as "position" and as "state" within the sphere of objective "circumstances" surrounding each object as its functional context (and felt within in the form of *Empfindnisse*), moving inward to the hyletic data that subsist in the reduced sphere of absolute consciousness, we have been finding an incidence of corporeity in each stage of the regression toward absolute consciousness. For Husserl the ultimate stage of phenomenological elucidation, in which the essence of the absolute will be scrutinized for itself, is effected in the reflection on internal temporality.

Consciousness as a synthetic operation that can intend ideality, identity, across a passing sensorial diversity becomes possible because it is the generation of a time field, primally produced by a time phase that retains past time phases and anticipates coming time phases. The retention and protention of time phases is the tension within the present of the "living now" which primally makes possible the intention toward identity that synthesizes the sensorial dispersion.[22] Identity arises in a conscious stream that holds its passage together.

The living now is the energy of the tensions of retention and protention, but Husserl conceives of the phase of the "living now" itself as an impression. The field of temporality is generated in a reciprocal implication of intention and impression.[23] The "life" or "animation" of the primary sensory contents is their continual survival in retentions of the phase of the "living now." The "living now" is an *Ur-impression* – the primal impression, the originative impression upon which sensory contents are imprinted and subsist. For the field of the now in which all that is given is given and all that is intentionally constituted is constituted, is unto itself a given. The substance of the mind is ultimately impressional in nature.

What is meant by speaking here of impression? To conceive the essence of the absolute sphere with the term "impression" is to conceive the substance of the mind as materiality and passivity, to conceive the absolute as fact and not as concept.[24] But it is no longer to think that the elementary mental event can be causally linked, as impression to impressor, effect to cause, with physical events; Husserl conceives of the primal mental event as an impression after the whole of the transcendent physical universe has been reduced. The "living now" which he calls an impression is not an effect of a physical process; it is that in which the totality of physical processes are constituted. It is an impression that is not impressed on any prior mental substance; it is, as it were, an impression that is its own substrate.[25] It "is the absolute beginning ... the primal source, that from which all others are continuously generated. In itself, however, it is not generated; it does not come into existence as that which is generated, but through spontaneous generation. It does not grow up (it has no seed): it is primal creation."[26] It is with itself that the impressional phase is linked, in the continuous differentiation of itself by which it originates its survival in retentions and its renewal in protentions. Thus the "living now" as impression is givenness, a "passive reception, which gathers in the novel, strange, and originary ..."[27]

3. Corporeal Intentionality

We have seen an inevitable corporeity come to light within the reduced sphere of "pure" consciousness itself. Corporeity here no longer means "extension" or "sensuousness"; it is a prenaturalized and unobjectified corporeity, whose essence is conceived as "kinesthetic sensations," "psychophysical state," "*Empfindnisse*," "hyletic materiality," and "impressional" nature of the now. The concept of corporeity can no longer be treated as a sub-species of the concept "thing."[28] But what, then, is absolute corporeity?

Merleau-Ponty founded his theory of the essence of corporeity in his early work on a transposition into corporeity of the movement of intentionality itself. He set out to show, in *The Structure of Behavior* and *Phenomenology of Perception*,[29] that intentionality, Heideggerianized as "existence," is enacted by body movement. Intentionality will be the concept that would make intelligible both bodily behavior observed physiologically and psychologically, and perception explored transcendentally. It was this thesis – and not the elaboration of a descriptive account of a dimension of corporeity lived in the first person singular, the "lived body" or "*corps propre*," distinguished from corporeity in the third person, the "objective body" – that was radical in his work. It is true that already for Husserl the ultimate substance of the mind is impressional in nature, and, since the whole hyletic layer involved in the constitution of objects is localized in *Empfindnisse*,[30] every intention aiming at objects is also a movement of orientation in regard to them. But Merleau-Ponty abandoned the conjugated hylomorphic-hermeneutic schemas of mental activity and transposed the format of intentionality into the essence of corporeity; intentional analysis now no longer operates within a metaphysics where consciousness is to nature in the relation of absolute and relative, origin and derived, but within a philosophy of nature where consciousness itself is produced by an "overlapping" of nature upon itself. Intentionality, which for Husserl was a transcending of the sensible – a meta-physical movement – Merleau-Ponty reformulates as a power of the sensible.

Merleau-Ponty has not come into this theoretical program as a result of a simple naturalization of the transcendental. By a more demanding and more theoretically reduced phenomenological description, Merleau-Ponty was led to a new vision of the ontological structure of sensible things.[31]

Suspending the terminology of facts and essence, sense-data and intelligible essence, qualia and eidos,[32] Merleau-Ponty subjects the sensuous aspect of things to scrutiny cleared of the sediment of metaphysical definitions. Contrast with ideal being had led theorists to ascribe to the sensuous an existence in the here and the now, the ineffable opacity of a presence that is total or null. But the properly sensuous aspect of thing is reducible neither to impression-atoms nor to qualia;[33] *Phenomenology of Perception* was to show the non-givenness, the non-givenableness, of such pure simples, the incomprehensibility of the very notion of impressions devoid of all structure and reference. What kind of being then do the sensuous moments have? Every description of them will state that the sensuous aspects themselves – the color, the tone, the odor – are *dimen-*

sional; they exist in trajectories of time and space and in depth.[34] In addition each has a kind of internal microstructure; red is not a blank opacity of a certain degree of density; it articulates a certain style or way of filling out, of occupying, its field – explosive, implosive, recessive, tightening, homogeneous or periodic, vibrant or absorptive, etc. Each is "a certain style, a certain manner of managing the domain of space and time over which it has competency, of pronouncing, of articulating that domain, of radiating about a wholly virtual center – in short, a certain manner of being, in the active sense, certain *Wesen*, in the sense that, says Heidegger, this word has when it is used as a verb."[35]

This insight into the inner being of the sensuous aspects makes it possible for Merleau-Ponty to conceive in a new way the *Gestaltung* that produces the coherence and cohesion of sensuous things. A thing is a set of sensuous aspects which each, in its own register of sensoriality, reflects the microstructure and style of all the others. One "manner of occupying space and time" – thinly, symmetrically, periodically, tautly, etc. – reverberates across the registers of sensoriality that answer to our sensorial samplings. The *essence* of the thing is itself sensorial. The essence of the lemon is not an ideal law deduced from its sensuous instances and conceived rather than perceived; it is the dense tightness of the seen yellow which already bulges it out for the touch that will make contact with its pulp and already announces its homogenous sourness to the taste (nothing that looks like that can taste crumbly or smell smokey). The essence does not have to be brought in; it is perceived with and in each sensuous aspect.

The essence is not only inner structure; it is relational; it is the referentiality of the inner grain of the sensuous aspect. It also refers by contrast to what is not itself. Merleau-Ponty was much impressed by Saussurian linguistics, and in his late work sought to express the relations between things and the relations between things and their meanings according to the model of the linguistic field analyzed structurally. The phenomenal field must then be conceived as a "diacritical, relational, oppositional system,"[36] which is "phrased" into things by systematic internal processes of articulation. Thus things do not take form about ideal poles of identity posited by the intentionality of consciousness, around which sensorial profiles would be assembled; they are engendered by the relief of the divergence each marks from the others – they take form by systematic lateral differentiation rather than by vertical identification. It is the lateral and oppositional relationship of one term to another that makes each of them significant, such that meaning appears at the intersection of and as it were in the interval between them.[37] Just as one does not learn the significance of language by learning the meaning of words one by one, additively, so one cannot apprehend the phrasing of the phenomenal field into things by "acts" which posit identities for them.

How then are such beings perceived? The sensuous data can no longer be conceived as ineffable moments of opacity reflected on the surface of the mind, or as matter formed by the mind. Each sensuous phenomenon is a distinctive articulation of a spread of space and a trajectory of time, and our sensibility receives the presence of the sensuous within itself by actively taking up its vibrancy and internal microstructure, actively conforming with it as upon a "ray of the world"[38] by eye movements, exploratory movements of touch, shiftings of the postural schema.[39] To see it is to see according to it, to see with it. *The sensuous is both what we see, and the dimension into which we see.* If the sensuous aspect itself is conceived as dimensional, receiving it must be enacted in a movement across space and time, by a motile body whose substance is able to conform to the style and grain of the things and thus receive within itself the patterning of their structures.[40] Such a sentient must then not be defined as the metaphysical opposite of the beings it knows (as subjectivity is defined by its opposition to ob-jectivity); it must be of the same sort as the being it knows, sensible like it.[41] "My body is to the greatest extent what every thing is: a *dimensional this*. It is the universal thing – But, while the things become dimensions only insofar as they are received in a *field*, my body is this field itself, i.e. a sensible that is dimensional *of itself*, universal measurant –"[42]

If the sensible knower is able to conform itself to one of the aspects of the thing, one of these "rays of the world," it already is in the presence of the thing itself. The thing is nothing but a configuration in which all the sensorial aspects implicate and express one another.

Transcendence is displaced, in Merleau-Ponty's conception, from being the defining characteristic of consciousness, intentionality, to the "flesh" of the sensible, for sensuousness is by being "always further on ..."[43] The sensible "is nothing else than a brief, peremptory manner of giving in one sole something, in one sole tone of being visions past, visions to come, by whole clusters."[44] We see, we touch the thing itself; the unity of a thing is not a presumption (*Meinung*) of consciousness, but is exhibited in the fabric of the sensible. The structural complex which is a thing, intersensorially observable, is not reached by an "interpretation" of sense data which would "adumbrate" it; it is not an ideal unity of aspects which would be reached by an intentional act transcending the sensible toward the ideal. For Merleau-Ponty the passage from one sensuous aspect to the thing itself is effected by the convergence of all the receptive powers of the body upon it. Such convergence is effected by the synthetic, or synergic, unity of the body-schema. "The whole Husserlian analysis is blocked by the framework of *acts* which imposes upon it the philosophy of *consciousness*. It is necessary to take up again and develop the *fungierende* or *latent* intentionality which is the intentionality within being. That is not compatible with 'phenomenology,' that is, with an ontology that obliges whatever is not nothing to *present* itself to the *consciousness* across *Abschattungen* and as deriving from an originating donation which is an *act*, i.e., one *Erlebnis* among others ... It is necessary to take as primary, not the consciousness and its *Ablaufsphänomen* with its distinct intentional threads, but the vortex which this *Ablaufsphänomen* schematizes, the spatializing-temporalizing vortex (which is flesh and not consciousness facing a noema.)[45] As the telos of the convergence of corporeal sensitivity, and not an ideal essence comprehended in its coherence, the thing-structure remains the term of progressive exploration; it retains its transcendence and its opacity.

The concept of intentionality one has is commanded by the conception one has of the internal structure of the object, the telos of intentionality. Merleau-Ponty describes the operation of intentionality as a receptive movement of a sentient being whose metaphysical constitution is like that of the being received – sensible like the world; intentionality (he rather says "existence") is enacted by body motility, it will be the very essence of corporeity. Merleau-Ponty's first two works endeavored to show that this is not only true of the corporeity discovered within, by transcendental reflection on the reduced sphere of absolute consciousness, but also true of the corporeity observed without, in the form of behavior opening upon a "world."

4. The "Mind's Body" and Nature

We have seen that the concept of intentionality, as exposed by Husserl and by Merleau-Ponty, requires a denaturalized, deobjectified conception of an "absolute" corporeity – the "mind's body" (*corps de l'esprit*). In both cases the "mind's body" is essential to the conception of the essence of mentality; the concept of intentionality is then not a "spiritual" or "mental" concept, and in conceiving the essence of consciousness in the notion of intentionality we do not conceive a mental activity which would then have to be linked to a body, by compound or by composition.

It is true that this corporeity is conceived differently by the two philosophies, and the difference is commanded by their divergent understandings of what is to be meant by intentionality. Husserl conceives the operation of intentionality, across a hylomorphic-hermeneutic schema, as a receptive intuition which synthetically posits objects by transgressing systems of data toward their ideal identities. The motility of the subject is involved in every coalescence of differently oriented sensuous patterns (*Abschattungen*). This conception involves corporeity under the concepts of the "position" and "state" of the subject, "kinesthetic sensations," "*Empfindnisse*," "hyletic data," and "impressional now." For Merleau-Ponty the apprehension of things, assuredly not a process of passive reduplication of their sensuous affects in a mental substance, is also not an apprehension of their ideal meanings for a mind; it is a captivation, in oneself, of their "manner of filling space and time," their sensible essence. Already the apprehension of any sensible phenomenon (and not only the apprehension of a sequence of differently oriented sensorial aspects) must be a movement across time and space, because all sensible phenomena exist in spatio-temporal "rays," are dimensional, and because to apprehend them is to capture in oneself the internal microstructure that governs their deployment.

We can break down the corporeal intentionality that sees the radiating sensuous tissue and sees according to it in terms of position, orientation, state of adjustment or maladjustment, contact, being moved and tension; we can then see this movement as a formative matter in a presence impressed on itself. Merleau-Ponty's movement from body-behavior observed externally to body-behavior reflectively intuited would thus rejoin Husserl's movement from a consciousness constituting all bodies before itself to a consciousness turning corporeally in the midst of the bodies it constitutes.

But a difference subsists – and it is ontological. To Merleau-Ponty it is unintelligible to attribute the power that captures the transcendence of sensorial world-rays to a being of a different metaphysical constitution than the sensible things; only a medium like the sensible it knows can capture in itself their essence and microstructures; "a mind could not be captured by its own representations; it would rebel against this insertion into the visible which is essential to the seer."[47] Then what we have called the transcendental or "absolute" corporeity of the mind is not to be metaphysically opposed to the corporeity (*Leibhaftigkeit*) of the things themselves, the corporeality of real nature: the "mind's body" is the inscription of nature within.[48]

This brings Merleau-Ponty to the view that consciousness is not enacted by acts and positings, but by intentional transgressions (*Ueberschreiten*) which are not the initiatives of an ego, but overlappings of "nature" – being – upon itself. The ultimate elucidation will have to take the form of a reflection on the primal unity of the "*natura naturans*" or being antecedent to the segregation into mind and into phenomenal nature, and on the internal radiation or "overlapping" upon itself upon which "acts" and "attitudes," including the "act" of intentionality, are founded.

In Husserl's ultimate intentions, the "corporeity of the mind" itself is to be suspended upon "acts"; hyletic data are to be shown to be constituted by the "longitudinal" system of acts by which consciousness is primally constituted as a time-field.[49] Thus the "absolute" corporeity discovered inevitably within the mind after all the reductions of nature does not have the sense of an inscription of nature within the mind: Husserl will maintain to the end the conception according to which the mind is to nature in the relation of absolute and relative, origin and derived, unity and difference.

The renewed, still more exigent, scrutiny of the given – of the sensuous – has, we have seen, led Merleau-Ponty to a new conception of intentionality. It is no longer, as for Husserl, a "metaphysical" movement transcending the factual, the sensuous, the diverse toward the ideal, the identical, but a "physical" movement in the sentient because he is of sensuous substance – a movement within his corporeality because it belongs to the physis.

This new concept of the intentionality within nature will lead to a new conception of the thought that reflects on it to formulate it. This thought is no longer essentially identification and predication, but interrogation. But to work out this interrogative essence of cognition will lead us back once again to the given nature – which we will find itself exists in the interrogative mode.

Notes

1. "Any perceiving consciousness has the pecularity of being a consciousness of the *own presence 'in person' of an individual Object* ..." Edmund Husserl, *Ideas Pertaining to a Pure Phenomenology and to a Phenomenological Philosophy*, First Book, trans. F. Kersten (The Hague: Martinus Nijhoff, 1982), p. 83.
2. Ibid., p. 124.
3. Edmund Husserl, *Ideen zu einer reinen Phänomenologie und phänomenologischen Philosophie*, Zweites Buch (The Hague: Martinus Nijhoff, 1952), pp. 120–25, 154–57.
4. Ibid., pp. 236–47.
5. *Ideas* I, p. 125.
6. *Ideen* II, p. 216.
7. *Ideen* II, pp. 167–69; *Cartesian Meditations*, trans. Dorion Cairns (The Hague: Martinus Nijhoff, 1965), pp. 50–51.
8. *Ideen* II, pp. 56–58.
9. Ibid., pp. 38–41, 158–59.

10. Ibid., pp. 57–58.
11. Cf. Emmanuel Lévinas, *En découvrant l'existence avec Husserl et Heidegger*, 2nd ed. (Paris: Vrin, 1967), p. 158.
12. Ibid.
13. *Ideen* II, pp. 63–64.
14. Maurice Merleau-Ponty, *The Visible and the Invisible*, trans. A.F. Lingis (Evanston: Northwestern University Press, 1958), p. 7.
15. *Ideen* II, pp. 65–75.
16. Ibid., p. 146.
17. *Ideas* I, p. 193.
18. *Ideen* II, p. 145.
19. *Ideas*, p. 204.
20. Ibid., pp. 240–75.
21. Ibid., p. 88.
22. It is the "longitudinal intentionality" which makes possible the object-constitutive intentionality. Edmund Husserl, *The Phenomenology of Internal Time-Consciousness*, trans. James S. Churchill (Bloomington and London: Indiana University Press, 1964), p. 107.
23. Ibid., p. 92.
24. "*Am Anfang is die Tat.*" Edmund Husserl, *Die Krisis der Europäischen Wissenschaften und die transzendentale Phänomenologie* (The Hague: Martinus Nijhoff, 1954), p. 158.
25. "An impression ... is to be grasped as primary consciousness which has no further consciousness behind it in which we are aware of it." *The Phenomenology of Internal Time-Consciousness*, p. 117.
26. Ibid., p. 131.
27. Ibid., p. 115.
28. "The flesh is not matter, in the sense of corpuscles of being which would add up or continue on one another to form beings. Nor is the visible (the things as well as my own body) some 'physic' material that would be – God knows how – brought into being by the things factually existing and acting on my factual body. In general, it is not a fact or a sum of facts 'material' or 'spiritual.' Nor is it a representation for a mind; a mind could not be captured by its own representations; it would rebel against this insertion into the visible which is essential to the seer. The flesh is not matter, is not mind, is not substance ... What we are calling flesh, this interiorly worked-over mass, has no name in any philosophy." Maurice Merleau-Ponty, *The Visible and the Invisible*, pp. 139, 147.
29. *The Structure of Behavior*, trans. Alden L. Fisher (Boston: Beacon, 1963). *Phenomenology of Perception*, trans. Colin Smith (New York: Humanities, 1962).
30. Thus all sensations are kinesthetic. *Ideen* II, p. 153.
31. "The Starting point = the critique of the usual conception of the *thing* and its *properties*

– critique of the logical notion of the subject, and of logical inherence – critique of the *positive* signification (differences between signification); signification as a separation (*écart*), theory of predication – founded on this diacritical conception" *The Visible and the Invisible*, p. 224.

32. Ibid., p. 130.
33. Ibid., pp. 131–33.
34. "Sensoriality; for example, a color, yellow; it surpasses itself of itself: as soon as it becomes the color of the illumination, the dominant color of the field, it ceases to be such or such a color, it has therefore of itself an ontological function, it becomes apt to represent all things (like engravings, *Dioptrics*, Discourse IV). With one sole movement it imposes itself as particular and ceases to be visible as particular." Ibid., pp. 217–18.
35. Ibid., p. 115.
36. Ibid., p. 213.
37. Maurice Merleau-Ponty, *Signs*, trans. Richard C. McCleary (Evanston: Northwestern University Press, 1964), p. 42.
38. *The Visible and the Invisible*, pp. 241–42, 218.
39. *Phenomenology of Perception*, pp. 208–212; *The Visible and the Invisible*, pp. 134–35.
40. "Between the exploration and what it will teach me, between my movements and what I touch, there must exist some relationship by principle, some kinship, according to which they are not only, like the pseudopods of the amoeba, vague and ephemeral deformations of the corporeal space, but the initiation to and the opening upon a tactile world. This can happen only if my hand, while it is felt from within, is also accessible from without, itself tangible, for my other hand, for example, if it takes its place among the things it touches, is in a sense one of them, opens finally upon a tangible being of which it is also a part." *The Visible and the Invisible*, p. 133.
41. "It is that the thickness of flesh between the seer and the thing is constitutive for the thing of its visibility as for the seer of his corporeity; it is not an obstacle between them, it is their means of communication." Ibid., p. 135.
42. Ibid., pp. 259–60.
43. Ibid., p. 217.
44. Ibid., p. 135.
45. Ibid., p. 244.
46. *Phenomenology of Perception*, pp. 322–27.
47. *The Visible and the Invisible*, p. 139.
48. "The meaning of being is to be disclosed; it is a question of showing that the ontic, the '*Erlebnisse*,' 'sensations,' 'judgments' – (the objects, the 'represented,' in short all idealizations of the Psyche and of Nature) all the bric-a-brac of those *positive* psychic so-called 'realities' (and which are lacunar, 'insular,' without *Weltlichkeit* of their own) is in reality abstractly carved out from the ontological tissue, from the 'mind's body' – Being is the 'place' where the 'modes of consciousness' are inscribed as structurations of Being . . . , and where the structurations of Being are modes of consciousness." Ibid., p. 253.
49. *Ideas*, p. 203.

CHAPTER THREE

BEING IN THE INTERROGATIVE MOOD

The different chapters of the fragmentary text of *The Visible and the Invisible* we have are structured into a polemic against empiricist operational thought, reflexive analysis, negativist, dialectical and intuitionist modes of thought; the work sets out to define an essentially, intrinsically, interrogative mode of cognition – a "question-knowing."[1] And throughout this work, Merleau-Ponty keeps up a polemic against every kind of positivism – the positivism of empiricism; but also that of reflective philosophy (with "all the positivist bric-a-brac of 'concepts,' 'judgments,' 'relations' . . ."[2]), the positivism of being in itself which is, in Sartre, the counterpart of the negativist conception of mind proper to dialectical thought; the positive essences presupposed by phenomenological intuitionism; and the positive intuition of immediate existence in Bergsonism. The ontology it was preparing proposes that being itself is not to be positively conceived, that "the existing world exists in the interrogative mode,"[3] "in a sort of gliding, beneath the yes and the no."[4] What could it mean to conceive being itself in the interrogative mode? What could be the purpose of such a project?

1. Perceptual Faith and Epistemological Skepticism

The first chapter of *The Visible and the Invisible* recalls the last chapter of Hume's *Enquiry concerning Human Understanding*. It concerns the origin of that vascillation in our relationship with being which is doubt.

Perception is contact with being; it is indeed the primordial contact. This contact elicits a kind of adherence, to which Hume already ascribed the psychological-religious term faith. Seeing is believing. To see is to see the things themselves; the world is what we see.[5]

But this faith is unstable. It is even intrinsically destined to break up; perception itself contests itself. Every appearance of being gives itself out as provisional, as subject to further confirmation; the definitive contact with being itself is "always further on."[6] "Everything that *is* could *not be*," said Hume, but that was for him a speculative fact; it meant that the concept of the inexistence of any being never involves logical incompatibility. Merleau-Ponty finds contingency in the immediate data, in the very intuitive appearance of existent beings; "each perception envelops the possibility of its own replacement by another, and thus of a sort of disavowal from the things."[7] The break-up of the perceptual appearances, their crossing one another out, their cancelling of one another,[8] continually disrupts the adhesion to the perceived elicited in the perceptual contact; the primordial contact we have with being is labile.

Doubt originates then in perception, and because of the nature of the contact with being effected in perception. The inconsistencies, discordancies, within the flux of sensible appearances prevent us from blindly trusting our senses alone, Hume says; we have to correct their evidences by reason.[9] The instability of perceptual appearances provokes us to seek fixed criteria of truth and error which have to be forged by the intellectual operations of reason; with the aid of rational criteria we seek to build up a system of propositions representing the universe of objects existing in themselves.

Yet, for Hume, this labor only issues in a new doubt – speculative doubt or posterior skepticism. Reason posits a domain of objects existing in themselves, to which our sole access is our uncertain perception. We can discount those factors in our perceptual experience which vary as our organs vary, we can strip the appearances of the secondary qualities, but that does not authorize us to posit the residue as representing the objects as they are in themselves. For we find that representations of the primary qualities of the objects take form with and through the secondary qualities, which we know to represent the way we are affected rather than the way the objects themselves are. And we are witnesses only of the representations that form and dissipate about us; we do not and can not witness the process by which they take form, by which they are allegedly caused in us by objects existing in themselves.[10] Belief in this causation sustains the rational labor to form discriminations within the dubious perception, but "the least philosophy" exposes the dubious moorings of this rational faith. "The 'natural' man," as Merleau-Ponty puts it, "holds on to both ends of the chain, thinks *at the same time* that this perception enters into the things and that it is formed this side of his body. Yet coexist as the two convictions do without difficulty in the exercise of life, once reduced to theses and to propositions they destroy one another and leave us in confusion."[11]

Hume finds again, then, in the order of propositions the same skepticism inevitable in the perceptual life; the order and coherence of our propositions turn out to be not more solid than the order and consistency of the things with which contact is made in perception. And yet generalized skepticism does not succeed in instigating in Hume a reflection on the nature of the being with which we have such dubious contact; thought, subjecting itself to critical self-examination and training itself in the mood of skepticism, continues to posit a world of objects existing in themselves, against which to exasperate its suspicion of itself. The moments of doubt occurring in the perceptual life – the "skepticism prior to study and philosophy" – concern the subsistence of the objects that appear; the Humean cultivated skepticism, posterior to science and research, is an incrimination of the "imperfection of our organs."

The Humean skepticism is hence an epistemological skepticism that tacitly contains an ontological dogmatism. Extreme attention to the manner of proceeding cognitively is accompanied by an eclipse of attention to the way of being of what is given or emerges primordially. The spontaneous belief in beings whose existence appears as the reason for and telos of the perceptual experience reappears, in the order of critical cognition, in the form of the protoscientific belief in pure objectivity, such that the reflexive and critical operation of cognition, "far from dissipating the obscurities of our naïve faith in the world, is on the contrary its most dogmatic expression, presupposes it, maintains itself only by virtue of that faith."[12] All the critical suspicion of modern philosophy is directed to the ways and methods of proceeding of the imperfect subject – "as if one already knew what to exist is and as if the whole question were to apply this concept appropriately."[13]

2. Perceptual Doubt and Ontological Interrogation

"For us the essential is to know precisely what the being of the world means."[14] The type of philosophy Merleau-Ponty wishes to inaugurate is one for which the doubt inherent in perceptual life provokes not a reflexive thought – a return of the subject suspiciously, critically, upon itself – but an inquiry into the meaning of the being with which contact is made in the uncertain perception. Merleau-Ponty is not simply searching for a new epistemological *method*.

The forms of thought successively examined in *The Visible and the Invisible* – the self-sufficient operational thought of positivist science, the reflective thought of criticist epistemology, the negativist thought of dialectical philosophy, the intuitionist thought assembling moments of insight into essences (phenomenology) or into concrete existents (Bergsonism) – are so many methods of overcoming the dubious perceptual experience, of making contact with an objectivity, or with a subjectivity, existing in themselves. They represent not so much different inquiries into the meaning of the world's being as methods more critical than perception to make contact with a being whose format has been presupposed. Merleau-Ponty's book first sets out to systematically cast into question the ontological presupposition of these forms of thought.[15]

But the form of thought *The Visible and the Invisible* intends to introduce is not entitled interrogative thought simply because it elaborates a polemic against other forms of thought which tacitly presuppose what the vascillations of perceptual faith should lead us to question – the meaning of the primary emergent being. It is a form of thought that discovers that *the existing world itself exists in the interrogative mode.*[16] This means that the distances and the vascillations and the negativity that make contingency be contingency and possibility be only possibility are in being itself and are not simply shimmerings of nothingness playing over the positivity of being due to the imperfection of our organs or due to the void in the core of subjectivity through which being is seen.[17] The discordance and contestation by which beings crowd out one another, eclipse one another and push one another into depth and into latency are not just contingencies of the way beings are seen by our imperfect organs, or by our insubstantial subjectivity nihilating itself continually; they are what makes beings be and be there.

The form of thought, then, that would discover and pursue the meaning, the plot, of being will have an interrogative form – but not because doubt would have forced it to recognize that it is out of contact with being; it is not a provisional state of expectation, provoked by doubt or by speculative skepticism, destined to be concluded and eliminated by positive cognition, by the epiphany of a plenary being that resolves all interrogation. We have to come to see interrogation itself as a form of knowing, a form of contact with being – and the maximal degree of contact. "The effective, present, ultimate and primary being, the thing itself, are in principle apprehended in transparency through their perspectives, offer themselves therefore only to someone who wishes not to have them but to see them, not to hold them as with forceps or to immobilize them as under the objective of a microscope, but to let them be and to witness their continued being – to someone who therefore limits himself to giving them the hollow, the free space they ask for in return, the resonance they require, who follows their own movement, who is therefore not a nothingness the full being would come to stop up, but a question consonant with the porous being which it questions and from which it obtains not an answer, but a confirmation of its astonishment."[18] While classical epistemology grounds its universalized doubt or its skepticism in the natural doubt inevitable in the course of experience that makes contact with being, Merleau-Ponty seeks to build an interrogative form of thought that would express and exhibit the interrogative scheme of the primary world horizon. 

3. Critique of the Epistemological Concepts of Faith and Doubt

Modern epistemology saw in perception a natural alternation of faith and doubt. Hume said that by "natural instinct" we believe in the existence of what appears in perceptual experience; by natural instinct and prior to all philosophy, all reflection, we believe in the real and doubt illusions. In *Phenomenology of Perception* Merleau-Ponty accepted the Husserlian terms *Urdoxa* and *Urglaube*: the perceptual experience is an apparition of sensible forms which elicit and motivate a "faith" or "primordial opinion."[19] To speak of "faith" means, he notes later, in *The Visible and the Invisible*, "an adherence that knows itself to be beyond proofs, not necessary, interwoven with incredulity, at each instant threatened by non-faith."[20]

Yet, in a note added to the first page of *The Visible and the Invisible*, Merleau-Ponty expressed a scruple: "the notion of fait has to be specified." There is in fact already something wrong in seeing in perception an alternation of acts of faith and of doubt. Faith and doubt are reflective acts, and in specifying the modalities of perceptual experience with these terms Hume and Husserl already introduce intellectual operations into perception.[21] This is patent in Hume, for whom the faith antecedent to philosophy is of the same order as the speculative or rational faith consequent upon critical examination, as the doubt from which philosophy arises – the antecedent skepticism – is of the same order as the doubt into which philosophy issues – the posterior skepticism. But "perception is not a science of the world, it is not even an act, a deliberate taking up of a position ..."[22] And perception is not contact with the true or the credible, but with the real – which is not the same thing.

To believe is to believe as true; to perceive is to perceive the real. It is true that moments of contact with reality, like moments of insight into the truth, are interconnected; the real forms a continuous fabric as the true forms a coherent system. But the solidity and cohesion of the real is not that of the manifest connections by which the true is grounded upon antecedents.[23] "My field of perception is constantly filled with a play of colors, noises and fleeting tactile sensations which I cannot relate precisely to the context of my clearly perceived world, yet which I nevertheless immediately 'place' in the world, without ever confusing them with my daydreams. Equally constantly I weave dreams round things. I imagine people and things whose presence is not incompatible with the context, yet who are not in fact involved in it: they are ahead of reality, in the realm of the imaginary."[24]

perceived world, yet which I nevertheless immediately 'place' in the world, without ever confusing them with my daydreams. Equally constantly I weave dreams round things. I imagine people and things whose presence is not incompatible with the context, yet who are not in fact involved in it: they are ahead of reality, in the realm of the imaginary."[24]

The perceived is not the grounded; it is not that which is manifestly consistent with its context of explicit connections and supported by its antecedents. It is not the true. It is not the ascertained, is not that which provokes in the subject the reflexive experience of certainty.

But the perceived is not then to be characterized as possible or probable. The perceived makes its appearance as a configuration of the world which awaits its confirmation from the subsequent flux of world apparition, and which contains in germ in itself a sort of intuitive potentiality for its own replacement by another configuration which would "cross it out" or "cancel" it. Afterwards, retroactively, "we seek in vain in this chalky rock what a moment ago was a piece of wood polished by the sea."[25] The index of reality that is invested in the new appearance is lifted from the prior one. This means, then, that this appearance and the one that will replace and cancel it do not have the status of successive possibilities, or hypotheses successively entertained, and that the appearance that was destined to be cancelled did not have the status of the "merely conceived," of simply subjective origin. It came forth from the world itself, as did the appearance that cancelled it, and each gives itself out not as probable but as real.

As the perceptual field then does not consist in moments of credibility, probability and improbability, the "notion of faith [has] to be specified. It is not faith in the sense of decision . . ."[26] It is not an act or an initiative; it is not preceded by a survey of the antecedents and the context; it is not a commitment to one hypothesis rather than to another.

Correlatively, when firm contact with the world begins to dissolve and gives way to the buzzing of phantasms,[27] when the movement of existence into the world reverses into a retreat to the margin of the world inhabited by the ghosts of things,[28] this is not acts of doubt replacing the natural instinct of faith. The monocular images which represent phantasms are not repudiated by an act of doubt in the passage to the binocular vision that reaches the real; they mature into the syncretic binocular vision, and are absorbed by it like residues of it or sketches of it.[29] What effects the passage is not an act of doubt provoking critical reexamination; it is the body which concentrates and centers itself.

Instead, then, of specifying, making precise, the notion of faith, explicating how seeing is believing, *The Visible and the Invisible* will abandon it in favor of the concept of an original interrogative relationship with being.[30] We will have to understand "perception as this interrogative thought that lets the perceived world be rather than posits it, before which the things form and undo themselves in a sort of gliding, beneath the yes and the no."[31] Interrogation is "the ultimate relationship with being" and is an "ontological organ."[32] Our primary contact with being is not belief in the manifest, the true, but "a continual enterprise of taking our bearings on the constellations of the world."[33] What is deficient in credibility is also something of being; we are offered not being itself, definitively, but rays, radiations of being, dimensions of exploration.

Determining perceptual experience as inaugural interrogation rather than faith and doubt requires now that the notion of interrogation is to be specified. This vital interrogation is not simply the alternation of expectation and satisfaction, demand and response, position and negation, affirmation and denial. Merleau-Ponty *opposes* it to dialectics. "The interrogative is not a mode derived by inversion or by reversal of the indicative and the positive, is neither an affirmation nor a negation veiled or expected, but an original manner of aiming at something, as it were a *question-knowing*, which by principle no statement of 'answer' can go beyond and which perhaps therefore is the proper mode of our relationship with being, as though it were the mute or reticent interlocutor of our questions."[34] This questioning is not a state of ignorance, void, nothingness, destined to be filled by the epiphany of the positive; it is the form of relationship with a world that forms and remains a horizon,[35] a field of contingencies, potentialities, perspectival deformations, "which thus is staggered out in depth, conceals itself at the same time that it discloses itself, is abyss and not plenitude."[36] Questioning then must be understood as the active manner of keeping in contact with a being that is and remains at a distance, contracts and dilates its presence, contests and negates its own course.

Questioning is not a state of non-contact, a negativity, due either to the absence of being, or to the subject first mired in its own nothingness – the phenomenology of questioning does not lead to an ontology of the subject as nothingness. Questioning is, to be sure, a state of "gaping openness"[37] about which a horizon of things recedes into distance and into indifferentiation. But this does not happen because, by moments, contact with being is lost (moments of doubt, of subjectivity cocooned in mirages created by its own spontaneity); it occurs because "he who sees is of [the world] and is in it."[38] "No question goes toward being: if only by virtue of its own being as a question, it has already frequented being; it is returning to it."[39]

It is the implantation of the seer in the world that makes the world appear to him as a horizon – that is, a field-structure where every surface prolongs itself into depth, where every configuration prolongs itself, in the expanse of time and space, into a dimension. It is the very force and evidence of this implantation here – a fact of concentration of existence, of ecstatic, diasporic existence having a site – that makes the distances, the distension, and the progressive indifferentiation of being manifest as such.[40]

This implantation is not immanence or mutual inscription. Idealism sees in the inaugural perception a consciousness constitutive of things; realism sees in it a consciousness simply receptive of the things. Both conceive of things as objects posited in perception, and both conceive of the perceptual relationship, when effective, to be one of adequation between subject term and object term. To conceive of the perceptual relationship as interrogative is to reject the concept of adequation at the basis of both idealism and realism;[41] it is also to conceive in an essentially new way the nature of the perceived field. To perceive is not to posit a term with which, then, the subject would be, due to its having constituted it or due to its having passively received it, in a relationship of adequation; perception is rather essentially differentiation, gradation, specification of distances, formation of tensions, reliefs, contrasts.[42] To not perceive something is not for a positive content to cease to be there before the subject; it is for there to be disarticulation, undifferentiation, for there to no longer be contrast, divergency, relief.[43] What we perceive then is not a positive term existing in itself and supporting its own "properties"; what we perceive is a contrast, a tension – not an adequation with our substance, but a difference from us, marked out in the continuous fabric of being, of "flesh," of which we too are a part. It is that divergency, that contrast, that is the perceptual meaning, the sense grasped in perception;[44] meaning has not a positive but a differential being.[45] For Merleau-Ponty the term interrogation was intended to name perception as an operation of making appear differences and distances. "We have with our body, our senses, our look ... measurants (*mesurants*) for Being, dimensions to which we can refer it, but not a relationship of adequation or immanence. The perception of the world and of history is the practice of this measure, the reading off of their divergency or of their difference with respect to our norms."[46]

4. Being in the Interrogative Mood

If perceptual experience is finite and ever non-definite, provisional – interrogative – if the world appears in the format of a horizon, a field of continually receding differentiation, this is not to be ascribed simply to the "imperfection and inexactitude of our organs." To do so is to maintain the regulative ideal of a fully positive and fully determinate epiphany of being in itself – a phantasm the Pyrrhonian paradoxes show us we must definitively reject.[47] It is true that our organs are imperfect and inexact, but being cannot exhibit itself and spread itself out without receding into horizons of indifferentiation.[48] How and why this is so is the central question of an interrogative ontology. We can note that Heidegger's work since *Being and Time* has been preoccupied by the effort to say what is this one movement by which being is simultaneously epiphany and occultation, by which it shows itself and hides itself. *The Visible and the Invisible* sets out to determine this movement in new terms.

What is at stake in the longest chapter of *The Visible and the Invisible*, that entitled "Interrogation and Dialectics" (at first sight a more developed version of Merleau-Ponty's political polemic with Sartre first argued out in print in *Adventures of the Dialectic*[49]), is the repudiation of the speculative concepts of position and negation, being and nothingness, for an interrogative ontology. Nothingness can only posit the positive being in itself; it cannot differentiate, grade, organize in depth and in degrees, into a plurality of planes.[50] The differentiation and occultation of being then is not a negative event; being is not so much hidden as harbored – delayed, postponed – by itself. But then we also have to abandon the idea of being conceived in the affirmative mode, the image of being that is projected as the self-subsistent correlate of our positive, lucidly grounded judications.

In *Being and Nothingness* Sartre had argued that what supports, what makes possible, the presence, the being-there-before-us, of sensible phenomena is being in self-identity, posited in itself. And existentialist philosophy was built on the interpretation of the essence of subjectivity as a movement of transcendence; subjectivity is existence *for* itself because it is first existence transcending itself – making contact with being outside of itself.

For Merleau-Ponty of *The Visible and the Invisible*, transcendence is the inner plot, the ontological format, of the things and not only of subjectivity. Transcendence is existing not in self-identity but in autodispersion; it is being beyond itself, outside of oneself, ec-statical. It is existing in multiple locations, not as a point-occupancy in space and in time but as a radiation, a dimension, a "world-ray"; it is not to be in-itself, but "always further on."[51] This bold transfer of the concept of transcendence from the analysis of the inner nature of subjectivity to that of the type of being constitutive of sensuously given phenomena "requires a complete reconstruction of philosophy."[52]

The Visible and the Invisible finds transcendence in its scrutiny of the mode of being of sensible phenomena.[53] The sense-datum is not a *quale*, "a pellicle of being . . . at the same time indecipherable and evident"[54]; it is rather a "certain differentiation, an ephemeral modulation of this world,"[55] a "punctuation in a field,"[56] that is, a hiatus, a caesura, a contrast, a "certain node in the weave of the simultaneous and the successive,"[57] a "quality pregnant with a texture, the surface of a depth, a cross-section of a massive being, a grain or corpuscle borne by a wave of being."[58] This is to say that the sense-datum does not exist in self-identity; it has the form of a dimension and not a point, a differential pattern across time and space rather than the factitial occupancy of a spot of time and space; it is utterly referential. It makes an appearance at a location only by forming, crystallizing or precipitating a medium.[59] And this is precisely what gives it its opaque, sensorial *presence*; "what is indefinable in the *quale*, in the color, is nothing else than a brief, peremptory manner of giving in one sole something, in one sole tone of being, visions past, visions to come, by whole clusters."[60] Thus "the sensible is precisely that medium in which there can be *being* without it having to be posited; the sensible appearance of the sensible, the silent persuasion of the sensible is being's unique way of manifesting itself without becoming positivity . . ."[61]

There is a reticence in the way beings become present to us, "as though [being] were the mute or reticent interlocutor of our questions."[62] With this form of being there can be no adequation, only exploration, solicitation.

To be sure there is a transcendency in the sentient subject; sensibility is movement from oneself to the being that presents itself. But this transcendence is not the ground of the presence of phenomena; it is itself elicited, sustained and continually provoked anew by the transcendence of things. Perception has the form of a questioning, a quest after things that are there from the start – from the beginning there is contact; they are where they are, but are also radially where we are, because transcendence is their being – but from the start recede in spatio-temporal trajectories, eliciting our movement after them.

5. Interrogative Ontology

The ontological discourse that thematizes the topology of a world existing in the interrogative mode shall have itself an essentially interrogative form. That does not imply that it shall be a discourse in the grammatical form of interrogative sentences, or be a systematic inability to make affirmations. It shall be a thought that says what it says not in formulas, where unknown terms are determined by relationship with known terms, and ideally in algorithm, but in an operative language which would express in its lateral movements, its metaphors, its transversal organization, the identifiable style, the structural laws, the regular relationships and the latent logic[63] of the things of the world. A true "coincidence, a manner of making the things themselves speak" "would be a language of which [the philosopher] would not be the organizer, words he would not assemble, that would combine through him by virtue of a natural intertwining of their meaning, through the occult commerce of metaphors – when what counts is no longer the manifest meaning of each word and of each image, but the lateral relations, the kinships, that are implicated in their shiftings and their exchanges."[64] It is assuredly a vast problem to set up such a form of discourse, and find for it criteria by which we can be sure it truly is "bringing the things themselves, from the depths of their silence, to expression."[65] Merleau-Ponty undertook this work in the fragmentary manuscript *The Prose of the World*,[66] by way of an extensive investigation into the origin of expressive forms.

This kind of interrogative ontology shall not be a foundation inquiry in the classical sense. Classical epistemology based itself on the doubt perception itself inevitably contains; by rendering that doubt reflective and systematic, extending it into a methodic doubt or a generalized skepticism, epistemology subjects the moments of dator perception to cross-examination, so as to provide for cognition truly credible primary data. It thus functions as a foundation for science, not to guarantee the methodological exactitude of scientific observation of phenomena, but to guarantee their status ontologically – their status as beings that can be credibly posited as existing in themselves. In doing so it contributed to building up a cognition that means to posit in the absolute our naïve faith in a world existing in itself.

The ontology Merleau-Ponty intended to build was not intended to secure data that would exhibit being in itself, to certify the naïve belief in the world in itself that positivist science takes up on its own account without dissipating its obscurities.[67] And yet contemporary science itself, in its operations on astronomical spaces and microphysical realities, as well as in its developments in the psychology of perception and social psychology, has learned to situate physically the physicist and to situate socio-historically the psychologist. In these developments, which Merleau-Ponty followed throughout his career, he saw an implicit abandon of the positivist conception of objective being which classical epistemology was intended to sanction. In restoring to view the total fabric of the brute world, from which our ideas of subjects and of objects have been lifted by abstraction,[68] the interrogative ontology will be able to show the origins of the "strangest" ideas of contemporary science[69] in our perceptual contact with being. Then in its own way the interrogative ontology will function nonetheless to illuminate the bases of science.

Notes

1. *The Visible and the Invisible*, trans. Alphonso Lingis (Evanston: Northwestern University Press, 1969), p. 129.
2. Ibid., p. 235.
3. Ibid., p. 103.
4. Ibid., p. 102.
5. "The problem then becomes one ... of making explicit our primordial knowledge of the 'real,' of describing our perception of the world as that upon which our idea of truth is for ever based. We must not, therefore, wonder whether we really perceive a world, we must instead say: the world is what we perceive." *Phenomenology of Perception*, trans. Colin Smith (London: Humanities, 1962), p. xvi.
6. *The Visible and the Invisible*, p. 41.

7. Ibid.
8. Ibid., p. 42.
9. David Hume, *An Inquiry concerning Human Understanding* (Indianapolis: Bobbs-Merrill, 1955), p. 160.
10. Ibid., pp. 161–62.
11. *The Visible and the Invisible*, p. 8.
12. Ibid., p. 15.
13. Ibid., p. 6.
14. Ibid.
15. "We must presuppose nothing – neither the naïve idea of being in itself, therefore, nor the correlative idea of a being of representation, of a being for consciousness, of a being for man; these, along with the being of the world, are all notions that we have to rethink with regard to our experience of the world." Ibid.
16. Ibid., p. 103.
17. "From the point of view of *Being and Nothingness* the openness upon being means that I visit it in itself: if it remains distant, this is because nothingness, the anonymous one in me that sees, pushes before itself a zone of void where being no longer only is, but *is seen*." Ibid., p. 99.
18. Ibid., pp. 101–102.
19. *Phenomenology of Perception*, p. 343.
20. *The Visible and the Invisible*, p. 28.
21. *Phenomenology of Perception*, p. 342.
22. Ibid., pp. x-xi. Cf. *The Visible and the Invisible*, p. 239: "One does not get out of the rationalism-irrationalism dilemma as long as one thinks 'consciousness' and 'acts' – The decisive step is to recognize that in fact a consciousness is intentionality without acts, *fungierende*, that the 'objects' of consciousness themselves are not something positive *in front of* us, but nuclei of signification about which the transcendental life pivots, specified voids."
23. The true is posited in "express acts which enable me to posit before myself an object at its distance, standing in a definite relation to other objects, and having specific characteristics which can be observed ..." *Phenomenology of Perception*, p. 343.
24. Ibid., p. x.
25. *The Visible and the Invisible*, p. 41.
26. Ibid., p. 3.
27. Ibid., p. 8.
28. Ibid.; *Phenomenology of Perception*, p. 343.
29. *Phenomenology of Perception*, pp. 230–35; *The Visible and the Invisible*, pp. 7–8.
30. "This indefatigable ranging over the things, which is our life, is also a continual interrogation. It is not only philosophy, it is first the look that questions the things." *The Visible and the Invisible*, p. 103.
31. Ibid., p. 102. "If we are ourselves in question in the very unfolding of our life,

it is not because a central non-being threatens to revoke our consent to being at each instant; it is because we are one sole continued question, a perpetual enterprise of taking our bearings on the constellations of the world, and of taking the bearings of the things on our dimensions." Ibid., p. 103.

32. Ibid., p. 121.
33. Ibid., p. 103.
34. Ibid., p. 129.
35. Ibid., p. 100.
36. Ibid., p. 77.
37. Ibid., p. 105.
38. Ibid., p. 100.
39. Ibid., p. 120.
40. "The visible can thus fill me and occupy me only because I who see it do not see it from the depths of nothingness, but from the midst of itself; I the seer am also visible. What makes the weight, the thickness, the flesh of each color, of each sound, of each tactile texture, of the present, and of the world is that he who grasps them feels himself emerge from them by a sort of coiling up or redoubling, fundamentally homogeneous with them; he feels that he is the sensible itself coming to itself ..." feels that he is the sensible itself coming to itself ... (Ibid., p. 113–14) In the constructive chapter "The Intertwining – the Chiasm" this becomes the central focus of Merleau-Ponty's revised phenomenology of perception – for, as he says, the principle fault of his *Phenomenology of Perception* was that it founded the analysis of perceptual experience on the concept of subjectivity, and not on the concept of implantation in the field of being. Cf. *The Visible and the Invisible*, pp. 183, 238–39.
41. Ibid., p. 103.
42. Ibid. "The decisive step is to recognize that ... the 'objects' of consciousness themselves are not something positive *in front of* us, but nuclei of signification about which the transcendental life pivots, specified voids ... the transcendent, the thing, the '*quale*' [having] become 'level' or dimension ..." Ibid., pp. 238–39.
43. Ibid., p. 197.
44. Ibid. "With the first vision, the first contact, the first pleasure, there is initiation, that is, not the positing of a content, but the opening of a dimension that can never again be closed, the establishment of a level in terms of which every other experience will henceforth be situated." (Ibid., p. 151) "The concept, the signification are the singular *dimensionalized*, the *formulated* structure, and there is no vision of this invisible hinge; nominalism is right: the significations are only *defined separations* (*écarts*) –" (Ibid., pp. 237–38).
45. Ibid., p. 235.
46. Ibid., p. 103.
47. Ibid., p. 5.
48. Ibid., p. 136.

49. "Sartre and Ultrabolshevism" in *Adventures of the Dialectic*, trans. Joseph Bien (Evanston: Northwestern University Press, 1973).
50. *The Visible and the Invisible*, pp. 68, 236–37.
51. Ibid., p. 195.
52. Ibid., p. 193.
53. Ibid., pp. 264–66.
54. Ibid., p. 131.
55. Ibid., p. 132.
56. Ibid.
57. Ibid.
58. Ibid., p. 136.
59. Ibid., pp. 132, 192.
60. Ibid., p. 135.
61. Ibid., p. 214.
62. Ibid., p. 129.
63. Ibid., pp. 100–101.
64. Ibid., p. 125.
65. Ibid., p. 4.
66. Ibid., Paris 1969.
67. Ibid., p. 15.
68. Ibid., p. 130.
69. Ibid., pp. 184–85, 225–26.

CHAPTER FOUR

INVOLUTION IN THE SENSUOUS

1. The Repudiation of Analysis into Sensations

The term sensation is ambiguous: on the one hand, to sense something is to catch on to the sense of something, its direction, orientation or meaning. On the other hand, to sense something is to be sensitive to something, to feel a contact with it, to be affected by it.

The level of sensation would be the original locus of openness upon things, or contact with them. But in classical epistemology, this layer also came to have the function of the simples, into which the complex acts of cognition could be etiologically decomposed. Sensation would be the stratum of here-and-now givens, facts, as opposed to the relations and references in which they could function as terms. It would consist in a multiplicity of impressions, points of impact or of contact. It would consist in moments of intensity, or qualities, taken without their quantitative extensions and relationships and their referential meanings.

For Merleau-Ponty the cause of phenomenology requires a resolute rejection of any notion of analysis into sensations. One cannot decompose the primary experience into meanings and impressions, structures and elements, relations and terms, complexes and simples. The concept of Gestalt expresses this indecomposability, where, although the whole and its properties are indeed seated in the parts and on the same level as they (not an ideal form imposed from without), the parts themselves derive their properties as parts and their very partitioning to the sites and roles they receive from the whole. A figure against a ground is already such a Gestalt – and it is the most elementary experience; to experience *is* to discern a figure against a background. What there is is not sensations which are then patterned or interpreted, but perceptions. Perceptions of things, and not of qualities or impressions. And the background that regulates the position and contours of the things is not a psychic space or empty field; it is the world-horizon, system of planes, levels, ordered gradation. The apparent sizes and shapes of fragmentary percepts, the sensory constants, the regulation of degree of illumination and tonal density – all this reveals, Merleau-Ponty set out to show in detail,[1] a telos of perceiving things in our perceptual life, and an imperative of compossibility and concordance of things. From its most rudimentary experience, our sensitivity per-ceives – goes out to, captures – things, and is open to *the world*. The perceiving subject has to be desubstantialized, and conceived as an intentionality, a self-transcending movement of ex-istence, and no longer as the place of inscription of impressions. The repudiation of all etiological analysis into sensations opens the field for the descriptive inventory of phenomenal structures – for phenomenology.[2]

But Merleau-Ponty came to present the perception of a thing not so much as a grasp of its form, contours or configuration, as a capture of its inner axes, the inner pulse with which it actively occupies its zone of space-time. The Gestaltist notion of structure is already, in the *Phenomenology of Perception*, being supplanted by a more phenomenological notion of essence – but essence as sensuous sense, described sometimes as a matrix or pregnancy, sometimes as an utterance. The water of the pool is present across the garden; "this red" is in fact a "punctuation" in the phrasing of a field, already an element of the *logos endiathetos*.[3] In *The Visible and the Invisible* the Saussurian notion of structure brings about a mutation in terminology with which Merleau-Ponty now describes the sensorial field; it is articulated not so much into terms, as into differences between terms. With its oppositional contrasts, its synchronic reliefs and diachronic recurrences, the conjunctive tissue of the sensible field is described as a text incarnating a wild, preconventionalized logos; the operational language, the speaking word, *la parole parlante*, is but the utterance of what the things silently mean – mean to say.[4] The silent world is already structured like a language.

2. The Motile Nature of Sensorial Intentionality

It seems to us that this phenomenology, making perception primary, veers toward a certain idealism. Is not something lost, in the measure that sensation becomes perception of a sense – that by which sensation is sensuous? The exposure to the field of the sensuous is not only a capture of messages things tap out on our receptors; it is contact with them in their resistance and materiality, being sensitive to them, susceptible to being sustained and wounded by them. Sensation also means feeling pleased, exhilarated, or being pained by the sensible. A sentient subject does not innocently poise objects about itself as its decor, it is not only oriented by their sense; it is subject to them, to their brutality and their sustentation.

Heidegger had used the idea of a projective prehension to circumvent both the idea of the primacy of sensations and that of the primacy of perception. The first contact with the world is in teleological and motile dealings with the instrumentalities at hand, and the comprehension it involves is not a subsumption under ideal identities of signification, but a power to take hold of possibilities with what is at-hand. However, Heidegger had thematized the subjection to the world, the being oriented, affected, attuned, disposed by it, the finding oneself in it and the being cast in it even as one distances oneself with regard to it and projects oneself into it, in the thematics of *Befindlichkeit, Geworfenheit* and *Stimmung*. It is true that there was still something ethereal in this sensitivity, for the Heideggerian affectivity is more a matter of being disposed by the layout of the world-clearing than a susceptibility to being gratified, exalted or pained by things. For Heidegger seats our vulnerability and mortality in our self-transcending and self-projective spontaneity, rather than in subjection to the contingencies and brutalities of matter. This sensitivity or susceptibility is conjoined with the comprehensive or comprehending thrust of the practical prehension of instrumentalities when Heidegger interprets them as dimensions of one temporal thrust. The being subjected to and affected by what has come to pass and the efficacious projecting oneself out to what is possible and to come are the two temporal dimensions in which presence to the real world is realized.[5]

In *Phenomenology of Perception* Merleau-Ponty sought to avoid the idealist character of the Husserlian, sense-ascribing intentionality by appealing to the Heideggerian concept of prehension. Things are com-prehended not when an identifying intentionality has supplied an identity with which to interpret their sensuous aspects, but when there is a "*prise*," a hold on them. Not only vectors of transmission of instrumental force, but the very sensuous materiality of things is given in a motor apprehension. The sensorial *quale* itself, the blue or the red, occupies its space with a certain condensing, radiant, recessive or rhythmic schema; and it is this inner movement or extensive essence which is captured by the abductive, adductive, or recessive motility of the sensitive organism.

The inner micromovement with which each sensorial consistency occupies its space is caught up in the motility of the exploring eye or hand, and communicated across the sensibility through the transversal unity of the corporeal schema. Thus the synthesizing agency is not the spontaneity of the mind, but the corporeal schema, which does not engender or posit the ideal term of their unity, but focuses upon a thing as upon a transversal unity of the different sensorial tones and textures concording, fitting together, expressing one another. The model is the way the monocular images are assembled into one visual objective: the agency that synthesizes the images on the two eyes into one transcendent object is a corporeal synergy which coordinates all the receptor surfaces of the body into one organ axed on the exterior pole. *The Visible and the Invisible* and *Eye and Mind* maintain this motor character of the intentionality in perception; the sense or essence of the water of the pool is sensed as the eye follows the way it holds and lets play the streaks of sunlight, the way it contrasts with the repose of the garden, the way its liquid undulations organize shifts of light and tonal contrasts across the field. This syrupy and aqueous essence speaks to the motility of our sensibility.[6] The impressional side to sensation is in fact this *being moved*. The grasp of the sense or essence involved is a capture of a schema of movement.

In *The Visible and the Invisible* the Saussurian way of describing the vectors of signification in the field of language supplies Merleau-Ponty with new terms and a new model for describing the sensible field. *Phenomenology of Perception* showed everywhere that the perception of things is not an interpretation of signs, an ascribing meanings to terms. But de Saussure's structuralism convinced Merleau-Ponty that speaking is not either – that the meanings are not deposited in terms, but lie between them, in either oppositions, and that the making of the verbal material significant is not a connecting it up term by term with an order of ideal essences, but an operating with these internal differences, a "gesturing" with them.[7] The way such a differential linguistic meaning is captured and conveyed in a speech act, or gesture, will serve as the model for the way a sense is captured in the motor intentionality of perception. No doubt this kind of "*prise*" – "hold" on to a difference – is going to be very difficult to describe; it is indeed inevitably going to be a different notion from that of the "*prise*" – "hold" that measures the sizes and orientation of things, hold that feels the throbbing or the rest in their colors – which the *Phenomenology of Perception* found in all kinds of sentience.

And Merleau-Ponty sought to restore its carnal and sensuous character, its sensitivity, to sensibility by a description of subjectivity as the locus where there is an overlapping or folding over of being upon itself. The sensible flesh can be a locus where all schemes and movements of things can be captured, not because it is a blank slate or hollow of nothingness and thus a pure receptivity, but because it already contains all that the visible, the tangible, the audible is capable of, being visible, tangible and audible itself. Itself a field where the sensible radiates and schematizes itself, it captures the patterns the exterior things emit on the variations or frequency modulations of its own body schema.

3. Subjectivity as Subjection

And yet how much still there is lacking in this account of the carnal contact with the world! Merleau-Ponty's carnal subjectivity figures as a measurant for the gradations and reliefs of a field, as the locus where the most remote radiations of the sensible are captured. But there is utterly missing that character of anxious and solicitous care for the world with which the Heideggerian *Dasein* was absorbed in its clearing. There is complete silence about what the late Heidegger felt compelled to thematize as the divine – that promise of sustenance and wholesomeness, that remoteness or sacredness that draws as it withdraws, and which is not a "value" which our own appraisal assigns to things, but the goodness of things by which they assemble us and are attractions – *Dingen*.[8] There is lacking, we can say, a substantial sense of things. To conceive of things as substances was not only to conceive them as substrates the understanding posits to support the attributes it predicates of them. It is also to sense what is supporting and sustaining in them, the sensible layout as a ground that supports our movements and our aspirations, and as a nourishing medium for life. And there is lacking a sense of the capacity to gratify us, to please us, to delight us and not only illuminate our understanding, and to pain us, which is involved in the sense of things as nodes of pregnancy and resistance. For to be sentient means that too: not only to catch on to their sense, but to be susceptible and vulnerable with regard to them, sensitive and subject to them. It is even in the midst of things – and not only in the projection into nothingness – that we are mortal. It is in our sensuality, our gratification and our pain, that we sense that we are mortal.

What is lacking in the phenomenology of perception is – sensation.

4. The *Apeiron*

The sensible field does not consist only of configurations against a background of potential things, or instrumental connections, or paths and planes. There is also an unformed prime matter. Sensibility occurs in a medium which is pure depth, but not empty space; filled with qualitative opacity. It has no contours, does not present itself through profiles, does not have sides, is depth without surfaces. It is neither delimited, nor positively without limit: it is indefinite, *apeiron*.[9] It presents itself through pure qualities, which do not qualify any substrate. Pure chaos, pure flux, it is present through incessant oncoming. It fills out a space-time presence, marks a presence with its density, through condensation and rarefaction, blotting out the wake of the passed through, obscuring the horizons of the future. In it all directions are equivalent and neutral; the present does not adumbrate the absent, the absent does not promise the present. It extends a sphere of presence, within which one can move indefinitely without diminution or loss. It has no orientation – no sense. It is not going anywhere. But it is immediately there.

Things take form neither in the emptiness of space, nor out of a field of potential things. Colors concretize in a chromatic medium, solids and vapors form in the density, sounds emerge in the sonorous element. "This red," Merleau-Ponty wrote, "emerges from a less precise, more general redness, in which my gaze was caught, into which it sank, before – as we put it so aptly – *fixing* it."[10] There was first this sensuous element, formless as a sea, dense as a sea, into which the gaze sank. The things do not crystallize along the axes of a space-time framework, or at the intersections of instrumental pathways; they solidify in a depth – in the day, in the atmosphere, in the density and din of the world.

The light is such a medium; it envelops us, and extends neither infinitely nor unto frontiers – nor does it have horizons. It dilates, fills a clearing, dikes off the darkness, which it hides with the incessance of its presence. The light is without parts, without sides, without contours, without profiles, without referentiality, without substance. It is like an adjective predicated of nothing. The night, opaque and full of the dark, is such an element, general thing that fills space, that draws one's gaze, one's hearing into its somber spaciousness without sites or axes. The ground is also such an adjective, a supporting without substrate, a depth beneath all things, sustaining every scene and every upright or unstable object, a presence everywhere felt, which one neither approaches nor withdraws from, since one needs its support in order to approach or pull back. Merleau-Ponty has himself said that the silence between particular sounds is not an auditory zero, like the soundlessness between colors; it is positive as the ground out of which or upon which the sounds come to posit themselves.[11] But this stillness is not a field or a dimension; it is a pure element, pure sensuous matter without form. The heat, the monsoon, is neither a thing nor a field for things; it is a qualitative intensity without structure, a clarity without distinctness, tropical element.

In *The Visible and the Invisible* Merleau-Ponty had learned, from Schoenberg, that all sensuous particulars of their own force of presence schematize themselves.[12] Ex-istence, that is, transcending one's here-now, becoming general, becoming a level or a schema or a dimension, is not only the property of the mind – or it is the property of the mind because the sensitive mind is sensible, and this schematizing oneself, this veering into generality, is the nature of all that is sensible. Points become pivots, lines become levels, planes become horizons. But in addition, things grasped, when let go, revert to the elemental.[13] The red of the blood, out of the excess of its redness, does not only become the level against which the other colors situate themselves; it becomes the element in which crimes, lusts, landscapes, wars, revolutions swim and are caught sight of. The solidity of the ground, paced off after the sea voyage, a crust, remains as the element in which solid things are posited. The savor of the wine turns into an element in which vitality surges. The sparkle of the day turns into a medium in which the look is buoyed up, borne from plane to plane, from visible to visible. In the core of the things one senses the element. One sinks one's teeth into the fruit, and discovers the nutritive element; one samples the liquid and joins the flux of the alimentary, general and undivided, a depth sounding into the sensuous.

5. The Involution of Sensation

How diagram the inner movement of the sensing of this sensuous element? The core idea in intentionality hardly suits it. There is not a positing of an ideal identity-term, maintained selfsame, to unify a multiplicity of sensuous givens. The solidity of the ground, the airiness of the atmosphere, the luminosity of the light, are not invariants, matrices of a system of profiles, or schemas elaborated in the reciprocal referentiality of sensuous aspects. There is not the tension of intentionality, not orientation, attention, focus. One finds oneself within the sensuous element; one does not have to aim at it or orient oneself toward it. Here one does not see why the essential would be in our motility; sensing the element is not a "*prise*," a taking hold of it; it would rather be a being taken, being held, or being taken in by it.

Here to sense is to sense the substantial. Not the substrate that supports the qualitative properties, but rather the qualitative properties found supporting oneself. The force of things is not only experienced as resistance, as exclusion, by which the thing is *partes extra partes*, and excludes us from its place and time. The forces with which we hold ourselves in our posture and exert our motility have incorporated the supporting force of the ground. This incorporation senses the ground. The look does not only probe with its own forces in a space emptied out by the light; in fact is not the space rather filled with the light, and the gaze buoyed up by this radiance and activated by it? Is not the chromatic field, intense or vague, more than an opaqueness that stops the ray of sight and encases in themselves the things it identifies; is it not also sustenance for sight? It is the richly colored zones, and not only the spaces between them, that elicit the look, that concentrates, fortifies and upholds it.

Not all the force prehended is formed in the synthetic unity of a posture or a gesture; there is a surplus – sensation glows in the surplus. This surplus vibrancy is affective in character; it is a feeling gratified, contented with a content. It was not preceded by a lack.[14] The sensation of light was not preceded by a longing for light, did not come to answer to a question or a quest.[15] The flux of the sensuous element piles up in pleasure, in the reflux of the first ipseity.

Husserl thinks that the nascence of subjectivity in sensation has to be conceived as intentionality, because he conceives of the sensuous impression as passing, already passing as soon as it comes, a point of plenitude (*Randpunkt*) already sinking away into emptiness;[16] the subject that receives it is already straining to retain it. The subject of the impression, then, the sensibility for it, is already retentional, retroactive, intentional. But the sensuous element – the light, the color, the tone of the world – is not a tide already passing, but an oncoming abundance. The relationship with the sensuous element is from within, and the ipseity in sensation should be diagrammed as an involution.

The pleasure of sensation is not identifying, neither in the sense of positing an ideal ego identity-pole to which to ascribe its differentiated temporal phases, nor even in the sense of directing itself back to itself as to one focus. To feel oneself sensuously contented is not to posit oneself, objectify oneself or identify oneself; it is not even to take up a stand, to stand in oneself. It seems to us striking that no one has noted that the pleasure of sensation, in its reflexivity or its ipseity, refracts each time, disperses, spreads, such that the one that is contented with the sensuous content is a labile identity. Merleau-Ponty emphasized that the apprehension of the color is immediately transferred across the whole body sensibility; the subject in Goldstein's and Rosenthal's laboratory who senses the blue before it becomes a visual datum senses it with a sliding movement across the whole body.[17] But when it is the blue itself, when the visual sensation is there, there is a feeling for the blue that closes in upon itself in this zone – and in this moment. The moments of sensuous content – and the ipseity in them – form moments of surplus – or pleasure – each a surplus over and beyond the forces comprehended in the stance of the organism, each a surplus beyond the others.

Against the empiricist conception of sensation, which conceives of the sensuous as a multiplicity of impressional points collected in the undifferentiated unity of a passively one psychic sphere, and against the intellectualist conception, which conceives of the sensuous as a manifold of givens synthesized by the original and originating identity of one ego, it seems to us that sentience is a manifold of points of ipseity contained in the undifferentiated unity of the sensuous element.

6. The Moral Taste of Sensuality

If sensation is the original subjectivity, it is because there is effected in it our original subjection to beings. *The Visible and the Invisible* conceptualized this by speaking of the sensitive being as the locus where there is a folding back of the world upon itself. This inscription of the world upon the subject is the very carnality of existence, the structure of flesh. Merleau-Ponty always sought to explicate it by looking at the overlapping of the visible and motor; the look that palpates the visible has already been imprinted with the pacing, speed and direction of its movement by the things it will see.[18] That is only possible because it is itself something visible, and it is its own visible being that extends outward in the field of movement, or the visible being of the field of movement that extends inward. In fact this continuity is realized by the movement, and by this imprinting.

But this imprinting of the movement by the moved cannot be conceived objectively, as a transmission of force in the continuity of a field already objectified. The continuity of the visible field of the world and the visible flesh is not itself something perceived or effected through perception, if it is what makes perception possible.

If this subjection to the world before it is objectified, this folding back of the world upon the subject before the subject unfolds the world about itself, is not of the order of perception, is it not rather, as Heidegger thinks, of the order of affectivity? Is it not felt in feeling oneself born, that is, given one's being, laden with it, afflicted with it, subjected to it?[19] There is something vertiginous in the weight of this being, fully, definitely, effected, which one can never get to the bottom of, or put oneself at the beginning of. This weight is felt in the effort to assume one's existence, to take it on or take it up, to appropriate it, and in the irrecuperable lag of this appropriation, always come too late, unable to exist the instant of one's birth. Across this feeling of the weight of one's own being, one feels the weight of the world in which it is deposited, and feels the weight of its beings.

But this lag is also what makes it possible for this being to be definitive. The imposition of being could be sensed only in a movement impotent in its regard, a movement that produces impotence. Such are the movements of a subject that exists only in engendering potentialities for existence, potentialities which are potential only by being possibly impotent – movements by which a subject casts itself into a field of possibilities which are possible only because they are possibly impossible. Indeed all of our movements produce anxiety, the sense of casting oneself into the emptiness, the anticipation of dying. It is by making itself a pool of anxiety that our existence makes itself subject to being, and the beings not only signal to us with their orientations, but weigh on us with their being, which is definitiveness and subjection itself.

In this analysis our feeling of having been born and our mortality enter into our sensibility as a subjection to the world. Our feeling for things is made of our stupor over finding ourselves born, and our anxiety over finding ourselves dying.

It does not seem to us, however, that anxiety – the being exposed to nothingness – itself elucidates the subjection being can be. In order to understand sensation as susceptibility, to be affected by beings, and by one's own being, is it not the capacity of being pained by things that should be explicated? Sensibility, as the capacity to capture the sense or orientation of beings, is also susceptibility to being afflicted by their force, sensitivity for them, capacity to be pained by them.

Pain seems to be completely immanence: pain is the experience of the contexture of consciousness by itself, according to the Sartrean definition.[20] Pain is wholly within the vibrancy of consciousness; an unconscious pain does not pain at all. The suffering of pain is a being passive with regard to oneself. To suffer the pain is to be unable to flee and to be unable to retreat, to know this impotence in a vain struggle to get out of oneself, to open wide upon the world, or to get back from oneself. One flees the pain by losing oneself in the spectacle outside, or, failing that, in making it a spectacle, retreating behind it to objectify it. To suffer is to find oneself mired in oneself.[21]

Pain then is the inner experience of one's own being as a weight, an affliction. The subjectivity that is susceptible of being pained is not one that stands in its own potentialities, in an ecstatic projection into distance, futurity, nothingness, but one that turns in being, in the definitive, the irrevocable. Pain is the inner sense of this irremissible bond sealed within the very capacity of subjectivity for its own being.

But pain is at the same time a strange evidence of the continuity of one's own being with that of the world. The plenitude, presence and force of being, with which a thing so securely is, within its own frontiers, is for subjectivity an excess – and strangely, one with the excess its own being is for itself. Mired in oneself one is also wracked to the world. But is it the world as such? That which afflicts and oppresses beyond one's own being is not the cosmos, the framework or the field, the universal and the necessary – nor the vectors of instrumental referentiality – nor the style of styles, horizon of all horizons. What wounds may be the instrument, but what pains is the sensuous element. In pain what oppresses is the light, the heat, the din, the density, the depth as such. In pain the sensuous is an oppression before it is a sense impression, impression of a sense. In this oppression being is not an instrumentality that imposes his stance and his posture on the user, or a content held that imposes its pacing, speed and direction on the movement that takes hold, but a materiality without form that wounds without informing, an opacity without sense, ends or end. And even the sensuous that contents pains. In all sensation our being exposed and vulnerable to, our being subject to the sensuous element is felt.

At the limit of pain there would be the prostration and agony in which dying is at work. Dying is anticipated in our existence not only in the anxiety which feels itself being cast adrift in the emptiness as it casts itself into the world; it is also anticipated in the agony which feels itself being crushed, prostrate, in a being turning more and more into weight and stupor. That being is one's own; pain is the inner travail of materialization. But the sense of mortality is not only the sense of being cast adrift in the emptiness, when the world withdraws. It is, in pain, the sense of being cast into the world, into the utter materiality of the sensuous element.

Notes

1. Maurice Merleau-Ponty, *Phenomenology of Perception*, trans. Colin Smith (London & New York: Humanities, 1962), pp. 299–334.
2. Ibid., pp. 56–57.
3. Maurice Merleau-Ponty, *The Visible and the Invisible*, trans. A. Lingis (Evanston: Northwestern University Press, 1964), pp. 131–32.
4. Ibid., p. 129.
5. Martin Heidegger, *Being and Time*, trans. John Macquarrie and Edward Robinson (New York and Evanston: Harper & Row, 1962), p. 177.
6. Maurice Merleau-Ponty, "Eye and Mind," trans. Carleton Dallery in James M. Edie, ed. *The Primacy of Perception* (Evanston: Northwestern University Press, 1964), p. 182.
7. Maurice Merleau-Ponty, *Phenomenology of Perception*, p. 183.
8. Martin Heidegger, *Poetry, Language, Thought*, trans. Albert Hofstadter (New York: Harper & Row, 1971), p. 174.
9. Emmanuel Levinas, *Totality and Infinity*, trans. Alphonso Lingis (The Hague: Martinus Nijhoff, 1979), p. 141.
10. Maurice Merleau-Ponty, *The Visible and the Invisible*, p. 131.
11. Maurice Merleau-Ponty, *Phenomenology of Perception*, p. 222.
12. Maurice Merleau-Ponty, *The Visible and the Invisible*, p. 218.
13. Emmanuel Levinas, *Totality and Infinity*, p. 133.
14. Ibid., p. 129.
15. Ibid., pp. 189–92; Emmanuel Levinas, *Existence and Existents*, trans. Alphonso Lingis (The Hague: Martinus Nijhoff, 1978), pp. 46–50.
16. Edmund Husserl, *The Phenomenology of Internal Time Consciousness*, trans. James S. Churchill (Bloomington: Indiana University Press, 1964), p. 95.
17. Maurice Merleau-Ponty, *Phenomenology of Perception*, pp. 209–210.
18. Maurice Merleau-Ponty, *The Visible and the Invisible*, p. 133.
19. Martin Heidegger, *Being and Time*, pp. 330–31.
20. Jean-Paul Sartre, *Being and Nothingness*, trans. Hazel E. Barnes (New York: Washington Square Press, 1977), p. 436.
21. Emmanuel Levinas, *Le Temps et l'Autre* (Montpellier, Fata Morgana, 1979), pp. 55–58.

CHAPTER FIVE

THE PERCEPTION OF OTHERS

We are in life all convinced that by opening our eyes and by listening we really do perceive other people.

It is true that I do not have immediate access to the conscious acts and states of others, nor to the ego identities that abide across the streams of their lives. And while we all perceive the world, the same world, I do not perceive the cross-section the world opens before another's eyes and touch. More directly I perceive the bodies of others. And as a matter of fact, I do not really experience the bodies of others as animate, alive, sensitive, motile in the sense that I so perceive my own body, and that each perceives his own body.

But still we are in life all persuaded that by opening our eyes and looking we see a human being there – not just colored patterns. We do not merely have a mediate, discursive idea of others; we do not merely posit their existence by inference, by taking certain sensuous data – in us or before us – as indications or signs of alien minds. For us other persons are not just hypotheses we entertain, or suppositions, or projections of ourselves. We do not just perceive sensible visual patterns, palpable forms, material bodies which look like other physical objects and might after all be automatons pushed by springs, covered with cloaks and hats. We are persuaded that in turning our attention to someone's voice, we are listening not just to vibrations in the air, but to our true love speaking, thinking, arguing, coaxing, teasing. In looking at another person's face we perceive his life; in touching another person's hand we touch his very sensibility.

By perceiving another person bodily before me, I recognize there a singular human, involving an animate body and subjective states and an ego-identity. Before this kind of mental performance, we can raise a transcendental question and a phenomenal question. What is the exact nature of the cognitive operation here performed? This question is raised from the transcendental point of view: it is not a question about the nature of an object, but about the nature of the subjective operations in which a particular type of sensible object is taken as known.

Our phenomenal question is: what is the justification for these cognitive moves, the motivations for them? Just what are the data sensibly given which justify the recognition of another man there? Just how do sensible appearances present a subjectivity to an outside witness?

We shall first examine the type of recognition-synthesis in which a sensuous experience acquires the meaning: another subjective being. We shall introduce a distinction between "identification synthesis" and "associational synopsis," in order to show how another can be perceived to be a human like me without my projecting my own subjectivity, or my concept of subjectivity, into him.

Then we shall address the problem of how subjectivity, conscious life, could be sensibly perceived. We shall examine first the question how I perceive conscious life in my own sensible body. We shall distinguish between two kinds of reflexivity, by which conscious life is given intuitively – what we shall call "immediate reflection" and "reflexive perception."

Then we shall show how conscious life is perceived – and not merely inferred – in the sensible bodily appearance of another. Here we shall introduce the concept of apperception, distinguished from factual apprehension and ideal constitution.

1. Subjectivity Generalized through Perceptual Assimilation

In order to determine first just how, in sensibly perceiving another, I recognize there another human, let us distinguish between two types of recognition which are effected in perception, the one built on the other. We shall call the one identification synthesis, and the other associational synopsis.

a. Identification Synthesis

The mind identifies something in the shifting flux of sensible patterns presented by the sensibility when it takes a succession of sensible patterns – differentiated in spatial position and layout, staggered across time – specifically as the manifestation of one and the same object. This operation effects a synthesis of a succession of sensible appearances.

And this active mental performance brings the mind into the presence of an object which transcends it. By taking each new appearance as a manifestation of one and the same thing, the mind maintains itself directed toward one selfsame term as the minutes pass, as the sensible patterns about it shift, metamorphose, pass. In this way the mind comes to experience itself not just in the presence of phosphorescent patterns which pass as it passes, and are thus correlates of the phases of itself, but rather in the presence of objects – terms that transcend the moment, that endure, that are more than any sense pattern affecting the mind at the moment.

Husserl originally understood intentionality, that is, the operation by which the mind relates itself to objects, to be this operation. Intentionality is active identification. The mind *constitutes* objects for itself out of sensible data not by a hylomorphic, or formative, operation, but by a hermeneutic operation.

For synthesis is not just coagulation, or material assemblage; it is unification in function of meaning. The relation between the given sensible appearances and the object they manifest is not a relation between parts and a whole; it is a relation between diverse sensible data and what those data are taken to manifest. The object itself, then, is: what these sensible data mean to me. It is the sense or essence or meaning of these appearances.

It is a term that transcends the particularity of the momentary sensible patterns, since they all manifest it. It is a constant or an invariant which subsists while the sensible patterns fluctuate. It is not itself strictly speaking given sensibly; it is the identity pole in terms of which the sensible appearances are synthesized; it is the term which makes what is given significant, recognizable, intelligible. Invariant and intelligible, it is ideal.

This kind of term, then, not strictly speaking sensible but intelligible, is not given to but posited by the mind.

b. Associational Synopsis

This account of the perception of identifiable objects – which invokes the classical, metaphysical, ultimately Platonic distinction between the sensible and the intelligible – is not by itself intelligible. For if the unity of the sensible appearances is not given to but posited by the mind, how account for the segregation of any particular multiplicity of sensible appearances for synthetization rather than any others? And if the intelligible identity of things is posited by the mind, how account for the emergence of one identity rather than another in any particular instance?

Before explicit identification can take place, it is necessary that a certain sequence of sensible appearances disengage themselves before the mind. They must stand out in relief. And they must be linked together, not by spatiotemporal contiguity only, but by immanent coherence, for even when their sequence is interrupted, they must be perceived to belong together.

The identity of a succession of sensible appearances is then not purely and simply posited by the mind, by fiat, to assemble a flux of sense data which of themselves are just a medly of sensations. The sensible appearances are already associated. An associational synopsis segregates one set of sensible patterns from the rest; within the associated set the presence of each brings out more strongly the contours and force of the others. At the same time there is a sort of contagion of meaning: the sense one appearance has spreads spontaneously to the associated ones in the sequence. In our perceptual life sensible appearances are continually and from the start given in such associational synopses.[1]

Association is not, as empiricism supposed, a sort of physical or psychic attraction due to spatiotemporal contiguity or similarity; it is due to a synopsizing operation of the mind. This operation proceeds not by positing an ideal essence and synthesizing the sensible forms as tokens or signs of that essence; it proceeds by instituting a sensible form and assimilating new perceptual forms with that one. The "institution"[2] of a sensible form that once passed before the sensibility is a retention of it in such a way that it functions as a sensible type, schema, or exemplar, and no longer just as a particular. The institution of a sensible type has thus to be distinguished from the simple persistence of an afterimage of an individual appearance in the mind – by which empiricism sought to explain associational unity without recourse to conceptual terms. To retain a sensible form specifically as a type or scheme is neither to perceive it in superposition on a subsequent particular form nor to abstract from it its intelligible essence. Thus a strain of music can be perceived as a variant of a prior melodic scheme, but that is not the same as conceiving, intellectually grasping, the system of relationships in which their similarity can become conceptualizable. Through institution sensible forms become sensible exemplars, points become pivots, lines become levels, facts become dimensions. Due to institution every new form is perceived specifically as a divergency from a prior form. The sensible form owes its relief then to the contrast it makes with instituted forms.

We distinguish then between identification synthesis, which is a true constitution of an object in function of an intelligible, or conceptual, term that transcends the sensible order, and which operates as a perceptual interpretation of the sensible in function of that ideal term – and an associational synopsis which proceeds by institution and assimilation of the sensible. Here the unity of a sequence of appearances is not a conceptual term posited by the mind itself; it is due to the institution of one appearance by a sort of dimensionalizing sensible memory. The identification synthesis takes each sensible appearance as evidence of one and the same meant term; the synthesis then is vertical, each sensible pattern linked to the next as so many parallel manifestations of an identity that transcends them and transcends the sensible order. In associational synopsis the synthesis is effected laterally, for each appearance is perceived as a variant of a prior one, contracting its sense by contagion, by spontaneous transfer. One might argue that one could not see one appearance as a variant of a prior one unless the identity of each were already disengaged, and that this occurs when an active initiative of the mind takes each as a sign indicating the selfsame identity term. We answer that the appearances must be already associated and seen as variants of one another if each is to be taken as a parallel token of the posited identity. And that therefore the assimilating perception precedes active identification. Perceiving each sensible pattern as a variant of another precedes seeing them each as indicators of an ideal intelligible identity.

If we admit this level of associational synopsis, then the identification synthesis becomes intelligible. For we now understand how a particular multiplicity of sensible appearances is disengaged to figure as a sequence, a system. And we can understand too how the ideal term each sensible appearance is taken to refer to is selected by the mind that posits it: the ideal, invariant structure used as the principle of identification is a conceptualization, a conceptual transposition and idealization of a structural unity already immanent in the associated sequence of sensible forms themselves.

c. The Analogizing Perception of Another

While looking at another sensuously – bodily – before me, I recognize in him a human, involving an animate body and subjective states and an ego-identity. The recognition involved here has been most often understood as an active identification synthesis. That is, I synthesize the sensible patterns before me by taking them as manifestations of humanity, whose essence is subjectivity. Subjectivity is not itself really perceived; it is rather posited by me in the measure that I take the sensible patterns before me as evidence of someone human being there.

But such an account is by itself unintelligible – in two ways. If subjectivity is just posited by me, in my synthetic interpretation of the sensible data the other's bodily being presents to my perception, then the origin of that concept of subjectivity requires explanation. Is it modeled after the subjectivity in me, and projected into the other? But it is *you* – an other – I recognize there, not my double. Is it modeled after my own subjectivity, but then generalized, such that what I conceive is a subjectivity in general, of which my own and that of the other are instances? But then my experience would not reach another individual subjectivity, a singular human.

Secondly, in this conception the relationship between the other's sensible appearance and his subjective essence is arbitrary. If it is the concept of subjectivity, posited by me, that is to first synthesize for me the sensible appearances his body presents and give them their animate sense, then those sensible appearances cannot by themselves motivate or justify one concept of subjectivity rather than another. What then proves to me that what I see is not just hats and cloaks covering automatons which move by springs?

These problems motivate us to search for a prior synthesis, an associational synopsis, preceding the identification synthesis and making it possible.

If we scrutinize our perception, we shall find an association – a pairing[3] – of the other's perceptible body with our own. The associational synopsis that prepares his sensible appearances for identification presents the peculiarity that it connects those sensible forms not only with one another, but also with the sequence of my sensible forms. Such that the perception of the other is an association with him.

My own body always figures, marginally, in my field of sensible perception – not, to be sure, as a material object, but rather as a volume of sensibility, of susceptibility, a sensation-zone in which representational and affective sensations are located, sensations of tone, pressure, buoyancy and fatigue, warmth and coldness, pleasure and pain. And since my perception is always retentive and anticipative, the field of my present sensations is always given in synthetic association with its past and possible formats. This sensation-field is synthetically one in a continuous associational synthesis, yielding that unity proper to a level of consciousness – ego identity: it is the field of *my* sensations. In addition this sensation-zone is a kinesthetic zone, a nexus of actual or potential mobile forces felt. Through kinesthetic sensibility my body space feels situated with respect to the field about me, and feels freely mobile in that field. Its present position and movement are kinesthetically felt to be associatively synthesized with its past and possible positions and movements. The pattern of internal kinesthetic sensibility is variable through volitional acts of the ego. It is the nexus of powers and habitualities which are *my* powers.

And because I feel myself to be extended and mobile, I can perceive my own body also from the outside; I can turn my eyes upon my own body, travel my hands over my own surfaces. I thus perceive myself as a sensible substance exposed to external exploration, set in a landscape of other sensible things – a landscape of things which I perceive in synthetic association with past and possible landscapes.

This perception I have of my sensible, bodily, form is constant – and is institutive. It institutes my own sensible form as an exemplar of living and sentient being.[4]

When the other is perceived, he is perceived in an assimilating or associating perception, as a variant of my own sensible, corporeal form. The sequence of sensible forms another presents to perception and the associated sequence of my own sensible forms seem to be similar, couple up, associate, each bringing out the contours and force of the other, the sense of the one set spreading to the other. They do not form one system of the manifestations of corporeality, but they do form parallel systems, the one progressively unfolding *as* a variant of the other.

So it is that I do not exactly look at the other's body; I rather look with it, pair up with it, I catch on to its axes of position, of direction, its manner of stationing itself before the spectacle about us; it looks to me like a variant of my own body. By a sort of extension of the anticipatory dimension of my own self-perception, I perceive the other's body as standing there where I could stand, assuming postures and positions I could assume, relating to the landscape about it as I could relate to it if I were there. Their sense then is associated, but within that associational synopsis the instituted archetype – which will be my perception of myself – and the variant will exchange their sense, and the transfer will not be one way only. To be sure the life I perceive in myself makes clear to me the sense of the behavior I observe in the other. But the forms of behavior I perceive in the other will also make the sense of my own behaviors clearer for me in turn. And thus this singular life can appear to me in its singularity, as a variant of the singular life in me.

How does this associational synopsis make possible and intelligible the synthetic act in which I identify the sensible appearances of the other's body as the manifestation of another consciously living member of humanity? First, it accounts for the immanent unity of the sequence of sensible appearances the other bodily presents. They are associated together, and are paired up with the sensible appearances of my body, and seen as a variant of it, before I posit subjectivity in them in an identifying interpretation.

Secondly, the subjectivity I recognize in the sensible appearances of the other is not my subjectivity simply projected in them, nor a generalized version of subjectivity conceptually elaborated and functioning as an interpretative principle. For my concept of his subjectivity is a conceptual expression of something perceived – a subjectivity perceivably animating his body, perceived as a variant of the subjectivity I perceive in my own body.

But what does it mean to perceive subjectivity in the sensible appearances another presents, as opposed to positing subjectivity for them or projecting it into them? First, what does it mean to perceive subjectivity in my own sensible body?

2. Immanent Reflection and Reflexive Perception

A body is animate, consciously alive, when it is sensitive to itself, feels itself, mobilizes itself, moves itself. Thus a reflexivity belongs to the essence of a body's being alive. This reflexive structure of life produces the primary experience of life: a consciously living being knows what life is first through the reflexivity in its own life. It thus follows that for it the prime exemplar of life is its own life.

And yet my experience of life can not be just an experience of my own life; there must be also an experience of another's life. For this to be possible it must be possible for me also to perceive life on the outside, in external perception.

Thus the experience of conscious life must be both reflexive and perceptual. And if the life I perceptually observe on the outside is seen as akin to the life I reflectively know in myself, then the reflexive consciousness of life and the external perception of it must not be experiences of two different types in alternation, but must be synthetically one experience.

Correlatively, if conscious life, which is reflexively known from within, can also be perceptually observed on the outside, then it cannot be just reflexively known in one mode – say, as force – and perceptually known in another – say, as form; its mode of apparition to reflection and to perception must be equivalent, must be synthetically one.

These exigencies bring us to reexamine the reflexive experience of consciousness.

a. Immanent Reflection

For the modern philosophical tradition stemming from Descartes, our immediate and basic experience of subjectivity occurs in an internal or reflective experience whereby I discover, by a sort of turning back of my own mental attention upon itself, that I am able to see, immediately, incontestably, that I exist at least as a stream of conscious states. Thought discovers that it always has this power to attend to itself; the mind has the ontological structure of existence-for-itself. For consciousness to exist is for it to be continually aware of itself, to be its own witness.

This reflexive experience is immediate and non-discursive; let us call it immanent reflection. There is an eclipse of the body functions and their interaction with the world; thought experiences itself directly, without the interposition of the body or the world, and even comes to wonder if it could then exist without the body and without the world. In turning back reflexively upon itself it seems to form a circuit with itself such that it not only becomes its own witness, but closes itself to outside observation. Its essential nature, which is to exist reflexively for-itself, is not mediated by anything extended or sensibly observable; the mind seems, then, not only to be its own witness, but to be its sole possible witness.

b. Reflexive Perception

But there is another sort of experience of my own conscious life I have. I am also reflexively aware of a conscious life in my body, animating my body. This means both that there is a consciousness in my body making my body sensitive, making parts of my body sense organs, and that conscious life mobilizes and moves my body. And that consciousness is my consciousness; I recognize myself in that body. I recognize the different parts and members of that body as belonging to me, as the different extended members of an ego-identity which is maintained across an interconnected sequence of conscious states. My conscious sensation-states are thus spatially locatable in my corporeal zone.[5] And I recognize not only that these parts and members "belong to me," but that they are animated by me, that my conscious operations make them sensitive and motile. How is this recognition performed?

Our thesis is that this reflection is a form of perception; we shall call it reflexive perception. It is not the immediate circuit that a pulsation of thought would form with itself, being given inwardly to itself. The interest of arguing this is that if I can *perceive* conscious life in my own body, I can also do so in another's body, and my experience of his life will be akin to that of my own.

My own body is given to me as consciously alive in two ways. On the one hand, it is given as a sensitive zone – a zone of susceptibility, of representational and affective, and also kinesthetic sensation. For my body as a sensation-field is always for me polarized by vectors of forces, axes of stance and of motility, kinesthetically felt: it is by moving my eyes that I see, and by moving my hands that I feel. Thus my body as a field of representational and affective sensation does not only give me the sense of what objects confront me and how they affect me, it also gives me the sense of how I stand and move in their midst.

On the other hand, my own body is something I can perceive by external perception: I can see most of it, I can touch one member of it with another, I perceive my body visually, tangibly, audibly, olefactorily. It is perceived specifically as a sensible object that is alive – and sensitive. In it my sensitivity is perceived in a sensuous form.

But just how is sensitivity perceived in the sensuous opaqueness of my externally perceived body? How does my sensibility reflexively recognize itself in that sensuous opaqueness? How are these two dimensions synthetically identified in this reflexive perception?

It is movement that mediates this identification. For if I recognize this hand I see, these eyes I touch, as alive, it is because I perceive ripples of movement in them. I perceive there movements of the same type as those I feel within, by kinesthetic sensation, movements taking form in that sensation-field which is my body-zone felt from within – movements that are spontaneous, ego-originating, and teleologically structured, goal-oriented. And even as I perceive my own body from the outside, my sensations of it are necessarily also kinesthetic – since I cannot perceive my body except by moving some of its organs over the others.

Then the hand that touches feels the touched hand to be another part of itself in the measure that it perceives in that touched hand a mobility of the same sort as that which it feels kinesthetically within itself. Movement is the common term that permits perceiving as synthetically one a sensitive zone and a sensible substance perceived externally, because I have a double experience of body movement. I perceive the movement visible or tangible in the palpable substance of my externally perceived body to be the same as, or to be a ramification of, a variant of, the movement I kinesthetically feel within.

Thus the perception of my own body by myself has a reflexive structure; as I perceive it I recognize the movement in it to be synthetically one with the movement with which I perceive it. In such a reflexive perception I perceive life *in a body*, conscious life *governing* a body, and recognize myself – my ego-identity – in that body.

3. The Apperception of Alien Life

Now the consciousness that recognizes itself in its own sensible form can recognize conscious life in the sensible form of another. The right hand that recognizes touch in the left hand it touches can also, by the same sort of perception, recognize touch in the hand of another. And so when I perceive the sensible body of another, it appears to me to be animate, sentient, self-motile, governed by acts of will, the carrier of an ego identity. If the other's body is associatively synthetized, coupled up with mine in my perception, inasmuch as it looks like a variant of mine, this similarity has to be not only in its sensuous qualities and quantitative determinations, but also in its looking alive.

The other's conscious life is perceivable in the form of the movements of his sensible body. These movements are perceived as 1) spontaneous, originating in that body itself, and not perceivably transmitted to it from the outside; 2) teleologically relating to certain objects and objectives in the world about him, a world I too perceive; and 3) consistent and coherent among themselves. Movements in different parts of the body, and movements at different phases of time, fit together, exhibit the internal organization of a common style. In the coherent style of the spontaneous body movements by which I perceive the other relating to the things about him I acquire a sense of his identity, that is, his ego governing in his body.[6] From within, he experiences his own ego as the unity or coherence of all his manners of relating to things, manifest in the system abiding across all his representational, affective, and kinesthetic fields.

The systematicity, teleological structure, and coherent style of the movement is no doubt not perceived in the sense that the color and form are perceived; they are not given in a spot of space or a moment of time. But they are coperceived with and in the sensuous quality and form. We can call this kind of mediate perceptual apprehension apperception.[7] No doubt it takes a synthetic apprehension to grasp the scheme, the style of the movement, spread out across space and time as it is. But the synthetic apprehension that grasps it is not an identification synthesis but an associational synopsis. It thus does not posit, does not constitute the unity of the succeeding forms, but institutes it.

Now in perceiving a body that is moving with this kind of movements, I not only seem to be perceiving a body that is moving itself, I also seem to perceive a body that is sensitive to itself. These movements seem to be the outer face of a corporeal zone of sensitivity, of susceptibility, a zone sensitive to itself. As I perceive them I have also a reflexive sense of a sensibility synthetically united with them. I then do not so much look at the shifting color patches and the contours; I sense the sensation, the susceptibility, the sensibility, I feel the mobility almost like I feel my own, from within.

Thus there is a reflexive structure also in my perception of the bodies of others. As I perceive their movements I get a reflexive sense of the sort of representational and affective and kinesthetic sensations with which those movements are experienced from within; I get a reflexive sense of what one perceives and how one feels affected and how one feels mobile in the course of such movements. They are synthesized with the kinesthetic experience I have of my own motility.

Why does this reflexivity operate in the case of perceiving the bodies of others, and not in the case of perceiving other sensible objects? Because the other's body is perceived as a variant of my own; the perception of another is association with him.

4. Validity and Limits of the Perception of Others

We can now raise the question of the validity of this experience of others, of this reflexive apperception of their conscious life – and by determining the limits of this analysis.

The conceptual instruments and the distinctions we have introduced permit us to produce an account of a veritable perception of another, such that perception does not give merely the sensuous qualities and form of the other's body, but gives that body as animate, involving subjective states and an ego identity. I perceive – or apperceive – the other's singular conscious life in his body just as I perceive my own conscious life in my own body externally. As long as we hold that my own conscious life could be reached only by an immediate self-reflective intuition, and the life of another is impalpable, and could only be formulated as a conception of mine, then access to my own life and access to the life of the others were essentially different acts, and the second could only be a projection of the first. But the conscious life animating the sensible form of another is not a simple hypothesis, or conceptual supposition; it is perceived, or apperceived, in the form of vital, that is, spontaneous and ego-originating and teleological, movement. The reflexivity by which conscious life is perceived in my sensibly perceivable body extends over to the other's sensibly perceivable body associated with it. On this basis I perceive not only how he is stationed in front of the things, but also how he perceives them and feels affected by them, and how he feels mobile and forceful before them.

The question of the validity of this perceptual experience of others can mean two things. Either it is a question whether the movement I see in another's perceptible body is indeed adequate evidence of the existence of an alien subjective life there. Or it is a question whether the concrete sense it has for me is the very sense it has for him.

Real existence of alien subjectivity – as of all sensible things – is the correlate of the continued concordance of the sensible patterns which is the evidence for it. And just as the continued concordance of sensible profiles continually confirms the existence and reality of the identity I see in them, so also the continued concordance and harmony of his gestures, stances, movements, facial expressions, which reiterate certain general patterns, which flow coherently into one another, which seem to manifest the unity of one style, continually confirms for me the existence and reality of the ego-identity I apperceive in them. The ego-identity of another is apperceived in the style his body positions and movements continually maintain. The moment this stream of behaviors breaks up into discordancy it begins to appear to me as a succession of mere spasms, and I lose the sense of there being an ego-identity immanent in them. And this body begins to appear to me as a pseudo-organism, a cadaver twitching due to local tensions, or a contraption, a department-store dummy, or robot gone haywire.

But the validity of the concrete sense his movements has for me is limited by the duplicity of the other's presence in the perceivable world. He has the power to deliberately deceive – to make movements in order to dissimulate his real perceptions, affections, volitions.

The type of account we have here elaborated seems to us limited in two ways. First, it would seem that the mind in the sublime sense

– the other's thought, judgments, decisions, evaluations, processes that have no necessary kinesthetic manifestation – escapes any perceptual experience. To the measure that that is true, they remain for me conjectures, suppositions of mine. They will have perceptual evidence for me in the measure that they govern his body, commanding his movements – both the movements teleologically oriented toward the objects about him, and also those movements directed, expressively, to me, making gestures and uttering the conventionalized sounds of language.

We have not, in this chapter, spoken about language. But language can be treated as a perceivable sequence of movements that reveal an alien subjectivity even while they convey ideal meanings. Our analysis can be fruitfully applied to this order of movements – conventionalized and expressive movements. We think it would resolve some difficulties of the Husserlian theory of expression, which seems to lead to solipsism. In the *Logical Investigations* Husserl treats of signs – and linguistic signs in particular – as having a dual function, to signify a meaning, and to indicate the mental states and acts of the speaker.[8] But his theory of expression not only fails to make comprehensible the connection between the two functionings of signs, but even makes their indicative function incomprehensible. For Husserl accounts for the meaning of expressions with a theory of what we have called identification synthesis, where it has to be me that posits the ideal meaning of the expressions and thus constitutes them as expressions.[9] If that is so, then the meaning the other puts in his expressions is not perceived by me, and his expressions do not offer any *evidence indicating* to me his *real* states of mind. We think the problem this raises is quite parallel to the problem that accounting for meaningful objects by identification synthesis alone presents.

But, secondly, it seems to us that a whole class of perceivable behaviors escapes the kind of analysis we have offered in this chapter. These are behaviors of the other which are of their nature *not* associated with mine, behaviors by which the other polarizes himself over against me. We are not so much thinking of simple opposition – for if a behavior is the simple reverse, or negation of mine, it can nonetheless be comprehensible in terms of mine, and in association with it. We are rather thinking of comportments by which the other situates himself over beyond me, below me or above me. These are the vocative and imperative dimensions of his behavior. They are moves – and perceptible moves – by which he does not associate with me, but situates himself over against me, opposes himself to me. To call upon me, to address me, is not to associate with me, to elicit my sympathy; it is to invoke me, question me, make demands on me. And to challenge me, judge me, command me, contest me is likewise to polarize over against me non-dialectically, irreversibly, nonsymmetrically.

We think then that there are forms of behavior that do not acquire their meaning for me by appearing synthetically associated with my behavior, appearing as a variant of my behavior. Forms rather whose sense is to dissociate with me. And what is striking is that these subjective moves, these forms of conscious life, are also perceivable. They are especially visible in the face of another – I see in his eyes that he addresses himself to me, invokes me, questions me, contests me. It is striking that my own perceptual experience of my own face – so vague, so inarticulate – is ill able to function as the type or exemplar such that the behavior of his face would take on its meaning for me in association with my own.

We think then that what we called the vocative and imperative dimensions of his conscious life – perceivable in his face and also in his language – requires a different kind of theory of perceiving the conscious life of another than the associational-reflexive theory we have elaborated in this chapter.

Notes

1. This was one of Husserl's theses: that an "intentional association" is at work everywhere in the first genesis of perceptual objects. Cf. Edmund Husserl, *Cartesian Meditations*, trans. Dorion Cairns (The Hague: Martinus Nijhoff, 1969), pp. 112–13 and 80–81. Cf. also Edmund Husserl *Analysen zur passiven Synthesis* (The Hague: Martinus Nijhoff, 1966), pp. 117–45.
2. The term is Husserl's; cf. *Cartesian Meditations*, op. cit., p. 111. But it was Merleau-Ponty who, in his late works, systematically contrasted the "institution" and the "constitution" of meaning. Cf. Maurice Merleau-Ponty,

Themes from the Lectures at the Collège de France 1952–1960, trans. John O'Neill (Evanston: Northwestern University Press, 1970), pp. 39–45, and *The Visible and the Invisible*, trans. A. Lingis (Evanston: Northwestern University Press, 1968), pp. 173, 217–19, 221, 244, 247.

3. As Husserl names it; cf. *Cartesian Meditations*, pp. 112–13.
4. The idea of the exemplarity of one's own experience of one's own body in perception was set forth by Merleau-Ponty in *The Visible and the Invisible*; cf. pp. 135–36, 145.
5. Edith Stein has very carefully specified the sense of "location" and the sense of "space" involved here in *On the Problem of Empathy*, trans. Waltraut Stein (The Hague: Martinus Nijhoff, 1964), pp. 38–45.
6. The thesis that the ego as externally observable is a stylistic and not conceptual unity was set forth by Husserl in *Cartesian Meditations*, pp. 119–20, and elaborated by Merleau-Ponty in *Phenomenology of Perception*, trans. Colin Smith (London & New York: Humanities, 1962), pp. 280–81.
7. As Husserl understands it, in *Cartesian Meditations*, p. 111.
8. Edmund Husserl, *Logical Investigations*, trans. J.N. Findlay (New York: Humanities, 1970), vol. I, pp. 269–98.
9. Merleau-Ponty set forth the principal objections to the constitutive theory of the origin of meaning in linguistic expressions in *Phenomenology of Perception*, pp. 174–206. In his *Speech and Phenomena* (trans. David Allison (Evanston: Northwestern University Press, 1973)), Jacques Derrida has exposed the difficulties in Husserl's conception of the connection between the indicative and the signifying function in linguistic signs.

CHAPTER SIX

THE VISIBLE AND THE VISION

What did Merleau-Ponty have in view when he said, with painters, that it is not I that see the trees and the landscapes, but it is the trees and the landscapes that look at me?

Phenomenology of Perception moved away from ascribing the look to an ego; vision must not be conceived as a succession of *acts*, initiatives, which are the work of an ego that identifies itself or posits itself in them. A look is a sort of motility that sees things by seeing with or according to the light, that lines up with the level of the light, and discriminates contrasts, degrees of divergence from that level. There is also another, lateral, attunement; each phase of a look takes form by varying a schema of vision already instituted, prolonging a seeing of the past. And taking up, prolonging, varying, schemata of seeing from the others. One picks up from others how to look for the leopard in the dappled depths of the rain forest, how to see the ribs of wrecks among the antlers of the coral cliffs in the indigo depths of the sea, how to see the force and the omen and the assignation in danses macabres of the African night where before, like Victorians, one had seen only crude and ugly carvings. There is an original intercorporeality, a "looking in general," which precedes and makes possible every moment of vision that forms in me and that focuses, that sees. Thus, in *Signs,*[1] Merleau-Ponty wrote that when I enter a room, I do not do so as an original constituting or synthesizing or formative, demiurgic, power, making a scene or a landscape out of what of itself is only hyletic data or amorphous sensory material. I enter a scene that is visible already, as though bathed immemorially by an anonymous and general look, and my eyes realize another variant or concretion of that look.

Eye and Mind goes much further, when Merleau-Ponty quotes painters saying that it is not I that looks at the trees, but the trees that look at me. There is no longer a duality of look in general and visible world – and my look and my radius of seen things as particularizations of the general confrontation; there is overlapping and reversibility of vision with visible. As when Heidegger writes that it is not I that speaks, but that words speak, or Being speaks, in me. My eye as seeing power does not double up, and superimpose upon itself my eye as a visible thing, but the visible field doubles up to inscribe itself upon that one chunk of itself which is my eye, making itself a vision on that visible. The visible organizes itself into a view, inscribes all of the visible, or some synopsis of it, on one of the visibles – my eye.

All this has a strange undertone of eroticism in Merleau-Ponty. In *Signs* he speaks of the Sartrean experience of looking not at things, at the eyes of another, but at his look; for Merleau-Ponty this does not yield, as for Sartre, an irreducible evidence of the ultimate ontological duality of vision and visible, subject and object. Each gaze caught in the other pushes against it without being able to turn it into an object, a visible, what it pushes against maintains itself as gaze and not visible surface – like the line of fire at the limits of erotic desire pushing against erotic desire.[2] The things seen are diagrams of one's own motility, the paths and planes delivered over to one's manipulation, and the intersensorial unity of the visible things is not that of a formula understandable or indeed posited in them by the mind, it is a unity forming across my own corporeal schema, my own intersensorial sensibility, it is the way this color is translatable into this tone and this textural value for my touch. The things are variants of one's own body, such that it is one's own body that is visible in them, such that vision is narcissism. But if it is in them that one's own body becomes visible or quasi-visible, it is they that make it a visible – such that one sees not the particularity of their visual forms and tones but their power to make visible, to make oneself visible, which is the second and more profound kind of narcissism vision is.[3] Sensibility is libidinal desire, libidinal desire is nothing else than our sensibility, for it is not objectification but incorporation, seeking of the outside within and of the inside without. The visible things take form at the joinings of our postural schema, in that inner circulation of intersensorial transpositions which is our dynamic body, they are "incrusted in our flesh"; but conversely our body sees when it exists in the midst of the visible, when it itself becomes one of the visibles, when the layout of the visible outlines as a visible thing in their midst one's own eye. When not only their diagrams are inscribed within, their intersensorial unity captured on one's own intersensorial unity, but also one oneself belongs in them, is fitted into them, becomes visible among them.

Lacan commented on these texts the week *The Visible and the Invisible* was published.[4] To give them a striking psychoanalytic interpretation, and transformation. Vision is non-coincidence; vision opens the outside world, travels it without harbor or rest for itself because the look does not see its own eye. The insatiable, ever transient look looks outside, goes ever further into exteriority, because it is originally exiled from the eye. The coincidence has been prevented, and prevented irremediably. But Lacan then goes on to say what the eye, that visible, is on the lookout for is not the (exterior) visible, but the look. What we are looking for is not raw hyletic material, or objective givens, but "a sight," "a view." When we look at a painting, what we see is not Mte.-St.-Victoire, but the painter's view. The look of the other. We don't see it, when we look at the canvas, but we do not look at the canvas to see the givens, the scabs of colored clay, either. We do not look at what is given. On the other hand, we do not look beyond them or through them for the real mountain in Arles that confronted Cézanne day after day. We look at the visible for the invisible – not the in itself behind the skin of appearances, and not the invisible which is the theme of the book *The Visible and the Invisible*, that is, the spaces between the trees, the lights and the shadows, the levels and the axes upon which the visible is set, where it concretizes as a contrast on a schema. The invisible we are on the lookout for is the look. That would not only be true when we turn our eyes upon canvases; it would also be true when we turn them on nature. When we climb a mountain, when we go climb Monte-Sainte-Victoire, it will be not in order to have the patterns of the trees inscribe themselves on the surfaces of the eyes as we climb; it will be to see "the view upon Arles from above," "the view from the cliff," the view from the pine trees – the valley or the clouds as seen by the trees. It will be in order to be the look the blind pines require. Lacan points out that in Sartre's famous first analysis of the experience of being seen, the example was not seeing the eyes of the other, but rather: hearing the rustling in the corridor and the footstep, the soldier seeing himself being seen by the light from the farmhouse on the hill, by the dense trees in the guerrilla and sniper infested woods. When we go down into the inhuman, humanly uninhabitable, unmanipulatable dephts of the sea, where we are no longer hands that form *Zuhandenen*, tools and implements, when we no longer can even retain the human upright posture or the swim strokes that propel humans across the surface of a pool, but are now reduced to being a visible in an alien, uninhabitable depth, nothing but eye, what we have gone down to the deep to find, what this eye is seeking, is not the colors and the patterns, the designs on the sides of the jackfish and the moray eels; we are seeking their look. I think every diver thinks the day he became a diver was the day he met the eye of the shark in its domain. To be seen by the shark, the lord, whose domain this is, that was what one went down there oneself to find. When one encountered the look of the shark, when one was oneself something seen in the domain of the shark. Longing to be the look the eye of the shark craves and requires.

The eye is not moved by an intentionality of need, but of desire, that is, by a craving terminated by no object that drives it far beyond the radius of the correlates of one's needs – unto the whole world. This insatiate desire is for Lacan the voluptuousness of the eye. The eye is a phallic organ; it is not on the lookout for things, for sense-data, for hyletic material, but on the lookout for a look, a look forever outside, exterior, the look of the other. The eye has been severed from its look, does not have, does not possess its look, which escapes it in exteriority. It makes contact with, caresses, but the visible – the other's eye. It accepts this original castration by seeking to be the look the other's eye craves.

The Lacanian appreciation in reality effects an extraordinary deviation from the Merleau-Pontyan text. For Merleau-Ponty if the look is not intuition but interrogation, this is not because it is irremediably castrated from its original object which is forever absent; it is because the being it interrogates itself exists in the interrogative mode.[5] The look is not an interrogation, a question, that would or could one day be resolved, an openness upon being which will one day be obturated by the plenary presence of what is given, it docs not open a blank which will one day be filled in by the response given by being, by being being given. That is because being gives itself only by allusions, in profiles, adumbrations; everything exposed occults all of itself but the surface of exposure, and occults other beings that sustain it, situate it and give it its sense. Every plenitude veers immediately and continuously into depth, into latency, into occultation, every diagram turns schematic, every fact is a transcendence.

But this depth is, in reality, on the side of the seer; vision inhabits the lights and the shadows, the spaces between things, the horizons. The invisible depth of being is the Seer in general. There are levels and schemata that make up the depth of the field, horizons, axes of continuation, and at any given moment the visible that takes form takes form by concretizing at an intersection of those lines of force, by diverging from the level or the schema, forming a contrast – by punctuating the phrasing of exteriority. The eye that discerns the divergence situates itself at the level, it sees with or according to the level, adjusts to the level. For example, it sees with, according to, the light, takes the color of the light as neutral for it sees the illuminated surfaces according to the degree of their divergence from the color of the light. The light guides the eye, like a look that precedes it, that probes the planes and apertures, that outlines the contours for the eye. "Our own vision only takes up on its own account and carries through the encompassing of the scene by those paths traced out for it by the lighting, just as, when we hear a sentence, we are surprised to discover the track of an alien thought. We perceive following the light, as we think following other people in verbal communication."[6]

Indeed the seeing of others is for us an institution of schemas and levels with which to focus our eyes, to direct and orient them, to move. We have learned to look from the way others look, as we have learned to assume a posture and mobilize our motility by capturing in ourselves postures and gaits of others.

For us to see, to form an act of looking, is to take up, modulate, distend the levels of the visible – and the look of another. The eye that looks at the green has to look at it with a certain focus, a certain restricted rubbing back and forth across its expanse, in order to make it visible; in doing so it finds it is not inventing a unique and singular act that for the first time makes this green visible, but is realizing one of a range of acts for which the grass is green, and thereby senses and sketches out other looks, looks of others, for which the grass is as green. A look from the first takes form as a particular on a schema of looking, a moment, a phase of a continuous seeing. And the momentary gaze makes itself schematic in turn; it outlines other focuses, other positions within the range of what makes the green seeable; it refers to the gazes of others, or to others as instantiations of the variants of itself. As it positions itself off another gaze, a gaze turned to another color or another green, it forms itself according to the gazes of others. There will be an equivalence of capturing the schema of a vision from the green and capturing it from the others.

The green becomes visible when its form, its expanse, its texture are translated within my body-schema into schemata of motility. The sense qualities and the shapes of the things convert into these diagrams of motility because they themselves ex-ist, that is, radiate themselves across space and time, schematize themselves, are transcendencies.

By inscribing their forms upon my substance, the things also inscribe my motility in the field of paths and planes, in contiguity and in proximity with them. I find myself in the midst of them, in the midst of the visible, myself something visible. I become something seen.

The color is in fact a radiation, the point becomes a pivot, the line a level, the form a plane. Particulars that of their own force prolong themselves across space and time, they are themselves movements. Tones making themselves felt across a field, punctuating the field of the visible, they simultaneously extend themselves and reverse themselves, positions convert into movements, facts into diagrams. Our own substance, then, sensuous itself as well as sensitive, is but a particular case, a pivot of the transcendency with which all that is visible, that is sensuous exists. It is a pivot sensuous thing in which all the surrounding things inscribe their dynamic diagrams, so as to activate and mobilize it. The painter walking in the forest feels within himself the schemes, levels, systems of gradation with which the contrasts form, the tones arise in relief, the things become visible being inscribed in his own substance. And he thus also feels himself being made visible, being woven into the fabric of the visible. His seeing sees by being guided by Sight in general, the invisible levels that make the visible visible, and they make him too something visible and seen. He can see a visible only by not looking at the light, at the levels, losing the initiative of his gaze to the invisible depth of the world, which sees with him and sees him each time he looks.

For Lacan, if there is desire, that is, not an appetite aroused by and gratified by the surface and the substance it finds within reach, not just need satisfied at the maternal breast, but desire for the mother herself, for the omnipotence the child wishes to subjugate to himself in the form of devotion, absolute love, there has taken form an object for desire which is unendingly removed from that desire. Desire is desire for the absolute, for infinity. Something has happened to the subject of needs such that he is no longer tranquillized, stilled, by any or all the objects that satisfy need. He seeks what is other than all those objects, and demands it of the other.

The Oedipus complex is the diagram of the process which transforms the infantile libido from primary process immediacy of gratification to a desire which is deviated, dispersed, articulated, regulated in the unending channels of civilization, that is, in the discourse addressed to the other. What is demanded of the child is castration. Both that he himself be severed from the organic unity he forms with the mother in the contiguity of immediate gratification, the tangency of the erotogenic zones, and that he be castrated of his own body qua pleasure-object starting with his penis. He must be skinned, stripped of that body, all surfaces, which is his flesh qua immediate pleasure-zone, erotogenic extension, and identify himself with the objectified body which is put before him by the mirror, and by those mirrors which are the gazes of the others.

This operation will be accomplished via the intermediary of the phallus. The child comes to take the castration threat seriously when he discovers the castration of the mother. And divines, then, both that he, who has come from that very place, that wound above her thighs, *is* the organ of which his mother has been castrated, and that that is the reason for her amorous desire turned on him. She has been fondling him, drooling over him, holding him up against her, with the integral, absolute, craving of love, as the prick which her mutilated body craves for its own integrity. He now divests himself of his skin, his body all surfaces qua immediate pleasure-zone, in order to project himself into this phallic image of himself he sees reflected in the mirror of her passionate gaze. He desires only to be the phallus his mother lacks. And with this desire he accepts to no longer desire to have the penis which is now barred from his body qua pleasure-object; he accepts the castration demanded. He invests himself no longer in his immediate surfaces, but in this phantasm which is not so much an illusion and an unreality as what is, what makes him be, a sign, addressed to the other.

The eye is a phallic organ, it is even the privileged organ by which the castrated child addresses himself to, invests himself in, what is apart, at a distance. It once existed as a primary process organ, organ for caressing surfaces, for being caressed by the surfaces, the phenomenality of the things; now it seeks the *objects*. That is, it no longer lets itself be caressed by the tones and the textures, the colors and the lights and the shadows, inasmuch as in their superfluity, their gratuity, they give rise to the production of surface pleasure, releases of tension, discharges and the death drive which seeks peace in them. Now beyond the surfaces it seeks the objects, that is, the visible inasmuch as it exists for the others, for anyone. It demands of each surface that touches it that it be an object, that is, that it capture the gaze of another. An object is ideal; it is the phantasmal image of the visible that the eye catches sight of in the gaze of another. And it is an ideal for the eye, the ideal the eye craves to be. The insatiable eye seeks to be those objects, and no longer to be caressed by their surfaces. It invest all its own reality in their ideality.

It seeks to give itself wholly to the gaze of the other, the mother, the lover. It seeks to be the visible, the eye, the gaze of the lover seeks across all the surfaces of the world. For it divines that the look of the other demands one's eyes. The searching, penetrating, captivating look of the other takes one's eyes, takes possession of one's eyes.

It is the other, who demands one's eyes, who holds one's eyes in his gaze, that effects the castration, the severage, the distancing of oneself from all surfaces that caressed the eyes.

The eye captures in itself the generating essences of the visible; the eye sees in the conjunctive tissue of things its own physiognomy; there is narcissism, Merleau-Ponty wrote, in all vision. But this narcissism is disclosure of the other in one's own closure; this eros is love of truth.

For Lacan the narcissism is alienation into the element of the phantasmal, dispossession and investment at a loss. The one that accepts castration, that is skinned of his body-surfaces as immediate erotogenic extension, to invest himself entirely in the visible in the mirror image of himself loses himself in this possession, is captivated and lost in the element of the other. The objectified body image he first recognized to be himself in a mirror – more exactly, the image which he does not so much identify, as the same as himself, as identify himself with, other in which he invests all of himself, this image is both his unreality and his ideality. It is henceforth as this ideal, this phantasm, this phallus, that he will circulate among the others.

What will be constituted as the visible for the eye – that erotogenic organ, that phallic organ, will be no longer the tones and shadows that caressed its surfaces. It will be objects, arrayed at a distance, captured in the mirror surfaces of their contours. The eye seeks these things. Not as the reality, the substantial essences, of the tones and shadows that once caressed it. As those tones and shadows projected on the phantasmal medium of that mirror that is the other's gaze. And as ideal – its own ideal. It projects itself into the visible objects, identifies with them. In order to capture the gaze of another, which both castrates it and reintegrates it into itself as that of which the other has been castrated.

The visible henceforth no longer separates – as for phenomenology – into the dispersion, the sequence of appearances, and the perceived objects that would be their truth and their reality. It rather separates into, on the one hand, a pure flux of phenomena without subsistence or identity, which gratify the sensuous surfaces of the eye, caress the eye, pass without having been identified, objectified or realized. And, on the other hand, a spectacle of objects, out of reach, out of contact, projected on the mirror surfaces of the other's gaze, phantasmal images without force. And which the eye craves not because they are real, but because they are ideal – its ideal. It craves them, craves to be them, not in order to be seen, but in order to be the seeing in them, the look the eye of another is on the lookout for. Craves to be the look of the trees, of the cliffs, of Mte.-Ste.-Victoire, of the coral reefs possessed by the eye of the shark.

We find ourselves thus on the brink of a question – wondering if a fateful preconception did not originally fix the sense of phenomena for phenomenology – that which sought their meaning in a problematic of truth and reality. Phenomenology refused to see anything in phenomena but exhibitions – exhibitions of reality that only wanted to show itself, and to be taken as it shows itself to be, wanted the way it shows itself to be to be the truth.

The meditation that follows not a will to truth in the eye but desire, eros, discovers a different function for the visible, and more than one. It comes to take phenomena, the colors, the shadows, as a surface phosphorescence, a gratuity, addressed only to surfaces, to erotogenic surfaces. The colors and the shadows that pass not in order to inscribe their truth, but to caress the erotic surfaces of the eye.

And the meditation on the desire in the eye will learn to take the objects, the visible things, fixed at a distance, not as the reality of those fleeting tones and shadows, but as their projection on the mirror of the alien look, pure signs of the non-integrity, the castration of the other. These object-objectives, nowhere visibly given, are ideal, the ideal the eye invests itself into, in order to be their look, the look of the trees, the cliffs, Mte.-Ste.-Victoire, the other, craves.

Flattening the surfaces of phenomena to the plane of reality and its truth, phenomenology loses sight of the other. This is particularly evident in Merleau-Ponty, in whom the sense of the other is very weak, and understood perceptually, as a variant of me – as my own stance or move that perceives is from the first a variant of a more general schema. The others, in Merleau-Ponty, occupy other sites on the levels and axes of the invisible with which I see. There is not, in his phenomenology, the other that can contest, that can demand, that can castrate me of my reality – that can imperatively require of me all my reality in order to overcome his castration.

Lacan's erotics is wholly commanded by such a sense of the other. The first meaning of alterity is the castrating father, the cannibalizing mother. Because phenomenology, and Merleau-Ponty in particular, envisages the other only as a variant of my perceiving, supplier of other profiles for my perceptual syntheses, maintainer of other sites with which I localize my percept, it fails to find the other in this virulent and irreducible mode of alterity. The child, dismembered and dissolute, disintegrated, born premature, who first saw in the mirror the eminently pleasurable and gratifying ideal of his future integration and wholeness, invested himself in that ideal only to lose himself wholly to the demand of the other. Who seeks in the infant only what is missing from his own integrity. Lacan knows intensely the appeal, the demand the other makes, his alterity is.

But there is something deeply unintelligible and incomprehensible in understanding it, as does Aristophanes in Plato's *Symposium* before Lacan, as an exigency for assimilation. If the appeal the other makes, the appeal his alterity is, is an appeal for the castrated part to be reintegrated into the original integrity, alterity subsists only as an exigency for its own undoing. If the demand that the other makes, the demand his alterity is, is a demand that the reality of the one upon which the demand is put be disinvested for the profit of the other, again alterity only subsists as the exigency for the same.

Lacan's erotics then contains an unstable and ambiguous concept of alterity. In the castration complex and the Oedipus drama it identifies the reality and force of alterity, the omnipotence of the other, as something appealed for and demanded. But do we not have to conceive alterity not as an appeal for completion, demand for one's reality for himself, but as the irreducibility of what is as an appeal, of what is as a demand? One would have to try to conceive of what it would mean for the other to figure as an appeal made to me that is not an appeal to exist as me – an appeal for the phallus I make of my castrated and dispossessed body. What it would mean for the other to figure as a demand put on me that is not a demand to exist as me – a demand that I be the look he lacks, a demand that he be the look I make of myself.

Reading Merleau-Ponty's *The Visible and the Invisible* with Jacques Lacan has enabled us to add to Merleau-Ponty's explication of the visible as reliefs on planes, divergent figures forming on dimensions, contrasts on inner and outer horizons, punctuations in the phrasing of the world-prose, the psychoanalytic perception of them as immediate pleasure-zone, erotogenetic surfaces that caress the eye. And has enabled us to add to Merleau-Ponty's account of the invisible as the depth of axes, dimensions, paths and lighting with which we see the erotic divination of a sight out there for which we long to be the organ. Merleau-Ponty's phenomenology does not have a virulent enough figure of alterity to explain how the primary visual palpation of surfaces gets severed from them and fixated on erotic objects, that is, objects of forever insatiable desire. But we think that Lacan's own concept of alterity is ambiguous in the measure that it figures as an exigency for completion, for absorption into itself of the castrated part. We think that when we locate that irreducible core of irremediable alterity in the other, then the object-essence of the objects we erotically crave in view of others who desire otherwise will also have to be defined anew.

Notes

1. Maurice Merleau-Ponty, *Signs*, trans. by Richard C. McCleary (Evanston: Northwestern University Press, 1964), pp. 15–16.
2. Ibid., p. 17.
3. Maurice Merleau-Ponty, *The Visible and the Invisible*, trans. by Alphonso Lingis (Evanston: Northwestern University Press: 1968), p. 139.
4. Jacques Lacan, *Four Fundamental Concepts of Psychoanalysis*, trans. by Allan Sheridan (London: Hogarth Press, 1977).
5. Alphonso Lingis, "Being in the Interrogative Mode," in Garth Gillan, ed., *The Horizons of the Flesh* (Carbondale and Edwardsville: Southern Illinois Press, 1973). pp. 78–91.
6. Maurice Merleau-Ponty, *Phenomenology of Perception*, trans. by Colin Smith (London: Routledge & Kegan Paul, 1962), p. 310.

CHAPTER SEVEN

INTUITION OF FREEDOM, INTUITION OF LAW

Phenomenology set out to make philosophy a positive discourse; all its statements were to be justified by the evidence of insights. Distinctive, then, to a phenomenology of action is the claim that there is something like an intuition of freedom. Freedom would be a given. The intuition of freedom cannot, to be sure, occur in a representational consciousness that represents the present, the hic et nunc, an empirical fact. It occurs in affectivity, it is an anxiety. Anxiety contains a non-discursive, immediate insight. It apprehends one's own nature as disconnected from universal nature, apprehends one's act, and, in Sartre's celebrated analysis of anxiety at the cliff's edge, one's subsistence, as not determined by the forces in the world.[1] It perceives in one's own present state causal inefficacy with regard to its continuation – one will have to conjure up an act in order to ensure one's being there in the next moment. It is at the same time insight that the goals that lure, those inactualities, issue not out of the plenum of the actual, but out of the gap between the actual and the future which our existence has to project itself across.

Kantian philosophy does not recognize this kind of negative intuition. For it intuitions are positive, positing; what is intuited is content, and forms. But there is also a primary and irreducible givenness of law. Law, however, not simply as form, instantiated in the recurrences empirical observation formulates. Law as force, as command – an imperative for laws. The imperative is a fact, is the first fact, for facts can be recognized as facts by a mind that thinks, that is, formulates representations of the universal and necessary.[2] This fact is a force intuited by an intellectual sensibility, enjoining the vital complex upon which it presses to make itself productive of acts that exemplify the universal and the necessary. The insight prior to all insights into facts is not an insight into freedom, but an insight into law.

The theoretical usage of reason does not simply respond to anthropological interests, but is commanded by the imperative, which commands a representation of universal nature such that all that is given is determined, specified and understood, through laws. It will also command man to represent his own given nature as a nature – a whole determined by laws – and an integral part of nature.[3] He will understand his physiological operations with the laws that are in effect throughout all physical nature, and that make the processes in his organism as predictable as the collisions of billiard balls and the movements of the stars.[4] A sector of his operations are mediated through representations. Psychophysiology will determine how sensuous representations occur on contact with trajectories of stimuli from external nature, and are efficacious to activate the motor system through the advance representations of pleasure or pain they contain.

The imperative is thus a force, and can generate the cognitive will that produces this determinist representation of nature and of one's own nature. But this supposes that the cognitive will is itself activated not by representations engendered on contact with external particulars, but by the pure intuition of an imperative for the universal and the necessary.

There is, however, no insight into the causal efficacy by which a representation formulated in obedience to the imperative for law determines the will and activates the nervous circuitry and musculature of our bodies (as there is no insight into causal efficacy in general).[5] The supposition of freedom – that the executive will and the physiological means it commands can be disconnected from the causal efficacy of the particulars of nature that press upon them – is not, however, just freely posited without intuitive evidence; it is commanded. For thought has to think that it can command its will so as to construct a representation of all nature according to universal and necessary laws. It has to think that it can will to think. It has to believe that it can command its will so as to subject itself to law, to be obedient.

Phenomenology claims to have isolated, through analyses of the cognitive value of nonrepresentational, affective, states, a primary and irreducible intuition into the empty locus of freedom. In addition phenomenology claims to have insight into the operations of freedom in the workings of the psychophysical agent. Like Kantism, for which the problematic of action is inseverable from that of cognitive initiatives, the phenomenology of action is but another formulation of the phenomenology of cognition, in particular, the phenomenology of perception. Sartre demonstrates that the body that manipulates implements is not activated in turn by mechanisms of the dynamic world, or of a psychic sphere, by showing that the manipulating hand is and can only be given as the focal origin of the lines of finality and of resistance that make the field a field of instrumentalities. Just as the non-perceptibility of the eye is a structural necessity of any visual field, where infinitely explorable realities are made to coexist in depth.[6] One cannot do what Kantism took the imperative to require – integrate the perceptible shapes of things, and the means-ends structures of implements of one's own perspective, and oneself, into a representation of universal nature. When the perspectival structure of the perceptual field and of the field of instrumentalities is reduced, so also the determination of shapes and colors, so also the practicable finalities. Once one sees the perspectival structure intrinsic to any cognitive as well as to any practical field, one understands the structural necessity of the perceptually inobservable observing body, of the unmanipulatable manipulator-body.[7] Here the intuition of freedom consists in recognizing the evident perceptual inexplorability of one's own sentient body, the evident non-manipulatability of one's own manipulating posture and hand.

Positively, the efficacy of this freedom consists in the power to posit goals, from which the instrumental organization of one's environs derives. Sartre's phenomenology of perception had shown that every perceptual determination of the given *this* as an identifiable thing is effected by a presumptive synthesis that posits the ideal totalization of the given along with the infinity of all the profiles it will or can show in the course of the exploration that takes it as real. When this presumptive synthesis is willfully altered, the future of the thing or of a layout of things is set forth as a goal of manipulative operations. Sartre's phenomenology passes over in silence, however, the problem, to Kantism closed to all insight, of the efficacy of this goal positing consciousness to activate the executive forces of the material body.

This intuition Merleau-Ponty's phenomenology aimed to supply, by describing a distinctive and irreducible perception of the body as a diagram of posture, a materialization of gestures, gaits, schematic movements. The axes of force of a posture are not determined by gravity, the schema of a movement not determined by the external force that disturbed the body equilibrium. The phenomenal body itself continually generalizes its particular positions into postures, stylizes its individual steps into gaits, schematizes the phases of its movements as soon as the limb begins to stir.[8]

Merleau-Ponty also deliberately brought together perception and action to the point where their analyses are inseverable. Perception is already action – since what perceives, what goes beyond the sensuous appearances to the intersensorial and constant *things* is not a purely intellectual operation of synthesis positing ideal identity terms, but a motor centering of the multiple surfaces of the sentient body on a term. It is the focusing of the two eyes that replaces the monocular images with one visual term; it is the integrated centering of the corporeal schema that posits the intersensorial thing as its correlate.[9] Per-ception as such is not intellectual identification added to sensation; it is prehension. Merleau-Ponty then did a micro-analysis of the process, not only showing that the objectifying positioning of a sensible thing as a whole in the field is effected by a centering of the whole corporeal schema on it, but that what senses, what captures a sensuous quality in any sense organ is not the specific chemistry of its substance, but an activity, a taking-hold (*prise*) by which the eyes that focus, the hand that fondles, actively takes hold of, and informs itself of the inner form, rhythm or grain of the expansive or recessive color, abrasive or slippery texture, thick or thin tone, vibrancy or resistance.[10]

If perception is motility, conversely action is perception. The hand that hails what looks like an acquaintance across the way disengages the familiar form from the crowd; the hand that reaches for the doorknob has already informed itself of the shape and final position of the objective from the start, and this perception is in each phase of the movement heading toward it.[11] To see something is to see how to reach it, and to reach for something is to perceive it, that is, to capture its form across the distance from the start. The freedom one intuits in perceiving one's own body, or the body of another, according to its postural axes, its gait, its schemes of prehension and avoidance, is everywhere in the perceiving organism. The perceived field – of which we cannot ask if it is real, for the real is ... what we perceive[12] – is the effect of this freedom.

And yet there is constraint everywhere in this world. The apparent sizes and shapes, colors and sounds refer to the real ones, those which are such as to compose a coherent thing constant in the variations of its settings. The things have to be compossible, the sensuous registers have to concord with one another, the horizon has to merge by continuous transition into the next horizon. One has to perceive things, has to perceive the world.[13]

But what then is this imperative to be in the world?

Sometimes this imperative is set forth as an essential necessity. As when Merleau-Ponty said that a figure against a background is not a contingent trait of perceptions, but is perception. It was his version of the dictum that every consciousness is conscious of something.[14] Yet these suppositions make us wonder if the aporia that says that the reflective procedures of phenomenology make prereflective experience the mirror image of the cognitive operations of reflection has been eluded by what Sartre and Merleau-Ponty have put forth as intuitionism.

For there is consciousness that is not conscious of some thing. There is sensibility that is not prehension of a form. There is sensuality in our sensibility, and of it Levinas has provided a striking explication.[15] Before sensiblity is perception, of forms, it is sensual, sensitive to matter, to substance. The things one does perceive one perceives in a medium to which one is sensitive – shadows and forms in the light, tones in air, solids held put and observable on terra firma, detachable, moveable things in the heat, resistances in winter, in the monsoon. The sensuous medium as such – light, darkness, the chromatic expanse, the solidity beneath the clearing, the density that fills it, the vibrancy – is not a multiplicity of discrete data, impressions made of messages tapped out on the membrane of our receptors. Nor is it reducible to properties qualifying the contours of things – things are found in the sensuous medium and not in the nothingness of empty space. The sensuous element is given without profiles, contours, surfaces, depth in which we find ourselves by being sensitive.[16] It is not decomposable into a multiplicity of potential profiles. It does not gradiate out in distances, end at limits or open in perspectival horizons; it is beginningless, endless, there by incessant oncoming. It is not negative, empty space, or the purely determinable of the Aristotelian physics – but positive, plenum, luminosity that fills out space, vibrancy that distends a sensuous volume, bottomless solidity of the ground not supported in turn upon which all things that can take form by occupying sites can be maintained in place.

Our sentient relationship with the sensuous elements is not an intentionality. One does not make contact with light by way of intentional synthesis of a given multiplicity of aspects or impressions, or by positing an ideal identity pole that would transcend the particular profiles offered. The sensuous element is not schema but substance; it supports us, sustains us, is sustenance, its content contents us. We can occupy a position, take up a stand, assume a posture because we are sustained by the solidity of the ground, our gaze buoyed up by the luminosity, our postural axis lined up with the vibrancy and materiality of the sensuous levels. It is not by ec-stasy, by intentional aim or by ex-istence, by projecting a goal or a future, that we make contact with the sensuous element, but in taking up a stance, in positing ourselves, standing in ourselves, forming an instant of presence.[17]

The contact is, to be sure, felt, and in the feeling is given to itself, is a consciousness. But this consciousness is affective and not perceptive, is pleasure or pain and not objectification. We enjoy the light, the heat, the solidity, the silence before we can – though we need not – perceive things and reach out to take hold of forms. The very forms and forces we grasp and manipulate revert, in the using, to their elemental essence; one enjoys the hammer in the hammering, the gaze tracking down things gets lost in the pleasure of the lambent spaces. The subjective movement in sensuality is not a transcending of the here and the now to the beyond – toward the sequence of the profiles or toward the ideal – but describes a movement of involution. There is not the freedom Sartre and Merleau-Ponty claimed to intuit in perception – ec-static thrust out of one's state of being, and beyond the actually given and presented object-objective; there is being-in one's own substance, insistance rather than existence, the involution of enjoyment in the medium in which one finds oneself.[18]

But action is demanded. It is by no means evident that it is generated simply out of pain, hungers, lacks that occur in the sensibility gratified from the first by the sensuous plenum. Action, the ordered assembling and adjusting of means in a practicable field, requires things, which require a world – and not only the immediate correlates of appetite, phantasms conjured up by hunger. Thus, as existentialism said, one has to be-in-the-world. One has to perceive things, prehend goals, form a world about oneself structured by a *logos endiathetos* by which everything is compossible. Why? What is this imperative that makes our existence a being-in-the-world? For Sartre and Merleau-Ponty this imperative is a fact whose imperative force they do not thematize. Kant did, understanding the imperative which makes us make our experience an experience of nature to be an imperative for the universal and the necessary, found immediate incumbent on the mind in its commerce with its own givens. It is then not things-goals that make one act; the imperative that one act, and not merely react to pleasurable or painful images, is shown to be also what makes us objectify the sensuous givens into things.[19]

The imperative is given, given to the sensibility, albeit a "sensibility of understanding," a purely intellectual and nowise sensuous sensibility.[20] The *phenomenon* of the imperative is not, however, the principles in which it is formulated and thus given form, represented by the mind. The formulation, the representation, is a product of the mind, whereas for the mind to recognize the imperative is for it to recognize its own dependence – the dependence of its spontaneous productivity on a force that binds it.

The real *phenomenon* of the imperative is what Kant calls the person,[21] that is, the other intuited as an instance of behavior regulated by inwardly represented law. This altogether distinctive intuition of the other's moves as diagramming a law he himself imposes on himself is opposed to the intuition of his psychophysical apparatus exemplifying the laws of nature. Respect for the other is respect for the law that rules in another, a distinctive intuition of the force in the forms of his behavior that commands me also.[22] One should not imagine that respect follows interpretation – that I interpret his positions and moves which I empirically perceive as instantiating a form of the law whose force I have known in myself, within my own faculty of reason. It is the reverse – I take the positions and moves of another, which are visibly interpretable as instantiating the ineluctable forms of natural laws, as instead instantiating subjection to principle his representational faculty finds incumbent on itself, because from the first I take the presence of another to concern me, to imperatively command me with whatever positions he takes and moves he makes.

For Levinas this Kantian intuition of the imperative is deformed by the idea, imported from the theoretical usage of reason (which, itself commanded by the imperative, is posterior to it) that the imperative is an imperative for the universal and the necessary. The force of the imperative has to be disengaged from this form with which theoretical reason interprets it – the force incumbent on *me*: an appeal that singles me out, a command that orders me.[23]

The face of another is the medium in which the imperative becomes evident, a phenomenon. Levinas showed how to separate the phenomenology of facing from that of things that shows their surfaces. In facing the other does not just expose a surface for our perception or a contour for our prehension. His exposure, a nakedness and a destitution, is an appeal addressed to us. He turns what is most vulnerable, the primal nakedness of his eyes, eyes that do not shine, that speak, that solicit, that seek out.[24] He faces with a word, which is not an arm, an instrument, which is the way to come disarmed and disarming. The words that hardly disturb the substance of the air, and are engulfed in it without leaving a trace, signal the other to us in his impotency, which we can resist without doing anything. He faces with a movement of his countenance, with a movement of his hand. Hands now that no longer grasp, take hold of the solid, that appropriate nothing, form the void. Empty-handed, the hands speak. To recognize the other that faces is to recognize that this appeal that singles one out does so imperatively, commands us. To answer to another, already to respond to his greeting, is to recognize his right to contest us, to make demands on us, to question us, to put our existence into question.[25]

The other does not command me by presenting me with a paradigm but by singling me out and appealing to me. The imperative is not an imperative for the universal and necessary; it is an imperative that I respond, arise and stand in the first person singular, to answer for his contingent and particular necessities, for his wants and failings.[26]

An appeal is addressed to one steeped in the resources of the sensuous plenum, whose egoism is an enjoyment. The response demanded is that one arise as a support for the weaknesses and failings of the other. The action that is imperative is not the Heideggerian manipulation that forms the exterior as means in view of one's own potentialities. Freud had shown that the first organ for giving is not the hand but the anus, and the first giving is not of one's things, detachables one has taken hold of, but of one's own substance.[27]

The position of being an agent does not arise in the midst of sensuous enjoyment, where cravings for substances lacking can torment one. It takes form when one perceives things as objectives, it arises in a world. We have argued that being-in-a-world, a world of perceivable things and prehendable objectives, presupposes subjection to an imperative. The subject as agent, subjected to an imperative, is a singular core of substance, of sustaining force, that can be employed for the support of another, that can be appealed to.

If I take myself not as a simple locus of intersecting currents of energy coming from the most remote corners of the universe and from time immemorial, but as a cause, a commencement, a source of resources, that is not the result of an intuition of myself as that supplement that makes a profile into a thing, a possible synthesis into a practical goal. It results from finding myself subject to an imperative. As Kant thought, the "I can" is given in an "I must." The constituting of the sensuous organism as an agent in its own right is dependent on the intuition of the imperative. The freedom of that agent is not given in a primitive intuition independent of the world or of the imperative that requires a world.

Notes

1. Jean-Paul Sartre, *Being and Nothingness*, trans. Hazel E. Barnes (New York: Washington Square, 1966), pp. 66–69.
2. Immanuel Kant, *Critique of Practical Reason*, trans. Lewis White Beck (Indianapolis: Bobbes-Merrill, 1956), p. 48.
3. Immanuel Kant, *Groundwork of the Metaphysic of Morals*, trans. H.J. Paton (New York: Harper & Row, 1964), pp. 88–89.
4. Immanuel Kant, *Critique of Practical Reason*, pp. 102–103.
5. Ibid.
6. Jean-Paul Sartre, *Being and Nothingness*, pp. 418–19, 426–27.
7. Ibid., pp. 428–29.
8. Maurice Merleau-Ponty, *Phenomenology of Perception*, trans. Colin Smith (New York: Humanities, 1962), pp. 450–52.
9. Ibid., pp. 230–32.
10. Ibid., pp. 209–10.
11. Ibid., pp. 137–38.
12. Ibid., p. xvi.
13. Ibid., p. 313.
14. Ibid., p. 4.
15. Emmanuel Levinas, *Totality and Infinity*, trans. Alphonso Lingis (The Hague: Martinus Nijhoff, 1979), pp. 135–40.
16. Ibid., pp. 130–34.
17. Emmanuel Levinas, *Existence and Existents*, trans. Alphonso Lingis (The Hague: Martinus Nijhoff, 1978), pp. 80–83.
18. Emmanual Levinas, *Totality and Infinity* pp. 135–38.
19. Immanueal Kant, *Critique of Practical Reason*, pp. 44–45.
20. Ibid., p. 75.
21. Immanuel Kant, *Groundwork of the Metaphysic of Morals*, pp. 95–96.
22. Immanuel Kant, *Critique of Practical Reason*, pp. 79–80.
23. Emmanuel Levinas, *Otherwise than Being or Beyond Essence*, trans. Alphonso Lingis (The Hague: Martinus Nijhoff, 1981), pp. 102–13.
24. Emmanuel Levinas, *Totality and Infinity*, p. 199.
25. Ibid., pp. 84–87.
26. Emmanuel Levinas, *En découvrant l'existence avec Husserl et Heidegger*, 2e éd. (Paris: Vrin, 1967), pp. 233–34.
27. Sigmund Freud, *Three Essays on Sexuality, The Standard Edition of the Complete Psychological Works of Sigmund Freud*, Vol. VII, trans. James Strachey (London, Hogarth, 1953), pp. 186–7.

Made in United States
Troutdale, OR
08/02/2024